MEDIEVAL WARFARE

Also by Terence Wise

Introduction to Battle Gaming
To Catch a Whale
Guide to Military Museums
Military Vehicle Markings
American Civil War: 1862
2nd Punic War
World War Two: Western Desert
American Military Camouflage and Markings 1939–45
Forts and Castles
European Edged Weapons
Polar Exploration
World War Two: Tunisia
The Peninsular War
Roman Civil Wars

Medieval Warfare

TERENCE WISE

Hastings House, Publishers
New York

First published in U.S.A. 1976 by
Hastings House, Publishers, Inc.

First published in 1976 by
Osprey Publishing Ltd.,
London WC2E 9LP

PRINTED IN THE U.S.A.

FOR SHIRLEY

CONTENTS

List of illustrations   ix

Acknowledgements   xiii

1   The Feudal System and Organisation of Armies   1

2   Armour   30

3   Weapons   67

4   Tactics   104

5   Castles and other Fortifications   134

6   Siege Warfare   161

7   Heraldry   183

Appendix I   Modelling Medieval Soldiers   222

Appendix II   Wargaming in the Medieval Period   232

Sources   243

Bibliography   244

Glossary   246

Index   253

ILLUSTRATIONS

Fifteenth century camp with baggage wagons, kitchens, amusement
 booths and camp followers (*British Museum*) 29
Short-sleeved German mail shirt, 1425–50 (*Wallace Collection*) 31
Pair of Milanese gauntlets, *c.* 1380–1400 (*Wallace Collection*) 34
Milanese barbute in Corinthian style, about 1445 (*Wallace Collection*) 43
Fourteenth Century bascinet from northern Italy (*Wallace Collection*)
 44
Pavises carried by a horizontal handle (*Wallace Collection*) 47
Italian bascinet, *c.* 1390–1400 (*Wallace Collection*) 48
Composite Gothic armour, 1470–1520 (*Wallace Collection*) 51
Gothic backplate of seven plates, *c.* 1470 (*Wallace Collection*) 52
Milanese globular breastplate, about 1500–20 (*Wallace Collection*) 53
German gauntlet, about 1480 (*Wallace Collection*) 54
Italian armet, late fifteenth–early sixteenth century (*Wallace Collection*)
 56
War-hat from Augsburg (*Wallace Collection*) 57
German sallet with visor pivoted at the sides, *c.* 1480–1510 (*Wallace
 Collection*) 58
German sallet forged from one piece, about 1450–60 (*Wallace Collection*)
 59
Nine chanfrons (*Grose*) 60
Horse armour worn up to *c.* 1400 (*Grose*) 61
Gothic war harness for man and horse (*Wallace Collection*) 62–3
Four swords, from *c.* 1340–1400 (*Wallace Collection*) 66
German long swords and a German sabre (*Wallace Collection*) 69
Sixteenth century falchion of Cosimo de' Medici (*Wallace Collection*) 70
Poleaxes of the fifteenth century (*Wallace Collection*) 75
Collection of maces and war-hammers, fifteenth–sixteenth century
 (*Wallace Collection*) 77
Fourteenth century axe-head and early fifteenth century mace-head
 (*London Museum*) 78
Late fifteenth century war-axe (*Wallis and Wallis*) 79
Selection of medieval spearheads found in London (*London Museum*) 80
Fifteenth and sixteenth century halberds and bills (*Wallace Collection*) 83
Fifteenth–sixteenth century daggers (*Wallace Collection*) 85
Cinquedea daggers or short swords from Ferrara (*Wallace Collection*) 86
Crossbow quiver of wood covered with rawhide, German 1470
 (*Wallace Collection*) 89

Breech-loading bronze gun from Turkey, 1464   95
Breech-loading peterara of forged iron, c. 1460–70   99
15-inch bombard, early fifteenth century, on a modern carriage (*Royal Artillery Institution*)   100
Order of battle for Byzantine cavalry (after Oman)   108
Crécy 1346   113
Agincourt, 1415   118
Morat, 1476   126
Grandson, 1476   127
The twelfth century castle of Loches, south-east of Tours (*French Government Tourist Office*)   137
The cylindrical keep of Gaillard Castle, built 1197–8   140
Plan of Gaillard Castle   141
The curtain wall of Pembroke Castle   142
Flanking towers in the east wall of Angers Castle on the Loire, 1228–38 (*French Government Tourist Office*)   143
Early fourteenth century barbican of Lewes Castle, Sussex   144
Caerphilly Castle, South Wales, late thirteenth century (*Crown Copyright*)   147
Queenborough Castle, c. 1361   149
Stahleck Castle, Bacharach-on-the-Rhine (*Embassy of the Federal Republic of Germany*)   152–3
Kalmar Castle on the Baltic (*Royal Swedish Embassy*)   155
The walls of Avila, north-west of Madrid (*Spanish National Tourist Office*)   156
The walls of Carcassonne, south-east of Toulouse (*French Government Tourist Office*)   156
The walls of Tenby, South Wales   158
The west gate of Canterbury town walls, 1380   159
Timber fort erected before the barbican of a castle, c. 1460–80   162
Trebuchet   166
A cat equipped with a ram   171
A belfry in action   173
A primitive siege tower (*Batsford Ltd.*)   175
Fifteenth century 'organ gun', bombard and mortar during a siege (*British Museum*)   176
Scenes of siege warfare (*British Museum*)   178–9
Siege scenes from medieval manuscripts (*British Museum*)   180–81
Heraldry
   Representation of colours   186
   Representation of furs   189
   The Shield Points, Divisions of the Field and Partition Lines   190
   96 examples of coats of arms   193, 195, 197, 199, 201, 203

24 coats of arms and crests   209, 211
18 livery badges   215, 217
14 examples of standards and banners   219–20

ACKNOWLEDGEMENTS

The author and publishers wish to thank the following museums and authorities for their assistance in gathering the illustrations for this book; the Wallace Collection and in particular Mr Vesey Norman; the British Museum; the London Museum; the Victoria and Albert Museum; Wallis and Wallis of Lewes, Sussex, auctioneers specialising in arms and armour; the Royal Artillery Institution; B. T. Batsford Ltd.; the Controller of Her Majesty's Stationery Office; the French Government Tourist Office; the Embassy of the Federal Republic of Germany; the Royal Swedish Embassy; and the Spanish National Tourist Office. The author also wishes to express his thanks to Furio Lorenzetti of Milan, who carried out researches into the *condottieri* and Italian heraldry on his behalf.

CHAPTER ONE

The Feudal System and Organisation of Armies

By 1300 the old feudal system of raising armies was break-ing down, but at that date – and for several centuries to come – no nation had sufficient financial resources to recruit, feed and pay a large standing army. Most governments of the 1300–1500 period lived a hand-to-mouth existence, scraping together a motley collection of fighting men whenever the occasion arose, often placing the king heavily in debt in the process. Therefore, the feudal system persisted in varying degrees in Europe throughout this era. Because of this, and in order to understand better what developed from it, the feudal system has been described here at some length.

The Feudal Tenure System

In medieval Europe land could only be held by possession or by tenure, possession meaning literally that the land belonged to whoever had possession of it, while tenure was the holding of a piece of land by acquiring the right from the possessor. Thus all land within a kingdom was possessed by the king, under God, and all other land 'owners' were but tenants to the king. The king retained large estates to provide himself with personal followers and royal revenues but the greater part of a kingdom was granted as fiefs to the king's great barons and church magnates, known as tenants-in-chief, in return for a commitment to supply a stipulated number of knights, who formed the backbone of a medieval army.

To raise this quota of knights the barons, bishops and abbots normally sub-let portions of their estates in return for the personal service of the sub-tenant, each of these portions being called a knight's fee. Often a fee incorporated a village, but sometimes one village might lie within the fees of more than one knight, and it was therefore divided into manors, the terms fee and manor eventually becoming synonymous. In French the knight's fee was a *seigneurie*, held by a *seigneur* – a lord, hence the term a lordship, also used for a fee. However, some tenants-in-chief, particularly church magnates and the German barons, preferred to maintain personal control over all their land and in these cases they supplied their quota of knights by having a personal following of paid knights, known as household knights.

Under the sub-tenant system each knight granted farms on his manor to freeholders on condition that they repaid him with goods or military service. The peasants, or villeins, worked the land under these freeholders, giving labour in return for the use of a strip of land. Therefore each manor was capable of providing a small 'troop' of soldiers, known as a retinue: the personal retainers of the knight and the freeholders fighting on foot, the knight's sons or younger brothers as men-at-arms and esquires on horseback, and the knight himself on a heavy charger and armed *cap-à-pied*. A retinue recorded in an English Parliament writ of 1277 consisted of twelve light horse, eight foot sergeants, one mounted crossbowman, six archers, seven boys with horses of low value and six men with axes and spades. Such retinues combined to make up the force required of the tenant-in-chief by the king, and the forces of all the tenants-in-chief made up the army of the kingdom – the feudal host.

The kings of most countries in Europe also had the ancient right to summon all able-bodied men to serve as foot soldiers in times of national crisis. This was the national militia, or shire levy; the forces of the shires under the command of their sheriffs. In England the right to call on all men between the ages of sixteen and sixty was exercised many times in the fourteenth century and was still being used in the late fifteenth century. The men were obliged to arm themselves in accordance with their wealth: men with 'chattels worth nine to 20 marks' had to have bows and arrows; men with '40 to 100 shillings of property' had to have bows and arrows and a sword; and men with an income of £15 a year had to serve on horseback. In Germany the militia, the *Heerban*, provided a reliable force of infantry, drawn mainly from Saxony and Bavaria and to a lesser extent from Swabia and Franconia. The soldiers were known as *Frîgebur*. The *Heerban* persisted much longer than the levies of most other countries. Similar systems for calling out the people *en masse* for the defence of the realm existed in France – the *Arrière-ban*, the Iberian peninsula and the Scandinavian kingdoms, but these forces were usually untrained and so poorly armed that they had no noticeable effect on the battles in which they fought.

Tenants holding less than a knight's fee were known as sergeants (*servientes loricati* or *serjans à cheval*) and these men were also called out in times of national emergency. Some sergeants had to carry a lord's banner in the field, or lead the local forces, but others were required to provide infantrymen, archers or crossbowmen, tenure by sergeanty apparently having a variable value. Sergeanty did not exist in England, although the term was used for fighting men.

In the past there has been some confusion over the term sergeant. Until the late twelfth century the term meant only a foot soldier, but from then on it came to be used more and more to distinguish the mounted soldiers from those mounted men who belonged to the knightly class. Sergeants are described as taking part in cavalry actions with the knights and it must therefore be assumed that they were armed with a light lance, sword and shield but that they and their horses were less heavily armoured than the knights. The fact that they were lightly equipped does not mean that they were light cavalry in the modern sense, although they were used for reconnaissance and skirmishing, but only that they were not so well equipped as the wealthier knights.

The term sergeant should not be confused with sergeant-at-arms, a rank originally implying membership of a royal bodyguard, formed by Philip Augustus of France for the Third Crusade. Similar bodyguards were soon adopted by other European monarchs and, because of their proximity to the king in battle, they were frequently used to carry orders, or see that orders were carried out. They were armed with a mace bearing the royal arms and this weapon came to be recognised as a symbol of royal authority.

The type of military service required of these various classes of fighting men differed somewhat. The shire levies could only be called out in time of national emergency and were under no obligation to serve outside their own country. In France the entire local force could be called out in defence of the duchy or county, but only a fraction from each could be summoned to serve the king. In England the levy served a maximum of forty days. Sergeants in Normandy served varying lengths of time: in France a period in proportion to their portion of a knight's fee; i.e. a sergeant holding half a fee served twenty days, a knight's period of service being forty days.

Tenants-in-chief were also rather restricted in the demands they could make on their vassals, a knight's service usually being limited to escort and guard duties, though in border areas the barons could call their tenants out at any time to repel raiders. Service with the army in the field was usually only demanded if backed by a royal summons, in which case the period of service for a knight throughout western Europe was forty days without pay in peace or war, with the possibility of longer periods being served with pay. Knights were also obliged to serve in the garrisons of royal and baronial castles and, although service in both the field and a castle was not really practicable, many knights found themselves obliged to fulfil both duties. The period of service in a garrison varied from two weeks to two or three months, the shorter period usually being served more than once a year, and a rotation of knights ensured the castle was always well garrisoned. However, if a field army was needed the knights on castle guard were frequently released from this duty, and in Germany, Normandy and parts of England and France their places were taken by sergeants and burghers (townspeople) who also owed castle guard service. Conversely, knights on field service might be sent to reinforce particular castles.

Northern France was the birthplace of this system of feudalism, which was carried to England, southern Italy and Sicily by Norman conquest. However, in other parts of Europe, although there was parallel development, the systems did not develop in an identical manner. In almost all other kingdoms, including France south of the Loire, some land remained free of any lord and the vassals swore only an oath of fealty – a promise to do no harm to the lord. In Russia, Scandinavia, northern Italy, Castile and Leon there were some feudal ties, but the system was never really fully developed in these countries.

Feudalism in the Fourteenth Century

Feudalism, the giving of service in exchange for land and the protection of a lord, persisted in parts of Europe until the late fifteenth century, but had degenerated considerably in western Europe by the end of the fourteenth century. Many minor offices, such as mayor of a town, or constable of a castle, or the taking of tolls on bridges and ferries, were now given as fiefs, and the money fief, or fief-rente, had been instituted, whereby military service was given in exchange for an annual fixed payment from the king. In part the degeneration may be blamed on the partition of fiefs and the resulting confusion as to who owed service to whom. This situation was caused by the division of a fief among the sons of the holder on his death, a practice originally forbidden. Prevention of fief partition made all younger sons landless, causing them to intrigue against the heir or leave their country to seek new lands, and therefore as early as the middle of the eleventh century fiefs began to be divided among the heirs. After several generations of such division the complexity of the tenures became so great that many knights held their fiefs from more than one lord, service being given to the principal lord, or liege lord. By the late twelfth century examples occur on the Continent of estates being divided into as many as ninety parts, with nine overlords: tighter control by the monarchy held off such a situation in England and Normandy for a longer time.

Scutage

Because personal service to every overlord was impossible, and because a fief might pass to an heiress or a minor unable to give military service, a system of commuting money for service, known as scutage or shield money, became inevitable. Scutage is recorded in Normandy and England as early as the end of the eleventh century, and in France by the twelfth century. By 1300 the system was in general use throughout western Europe and scutage was demanded by the king whenever a campaign was being prepared, peace-time service having ceased to be compulsory. The scutage was paid to the king by his tenants-in-chief, who collected it from their vassals; not just the lords of the fiefs but also those who held part of a fief. However, the cost of hiring a knight doubled between the late twelfth and early thirteenth centuries and this, together with the partition of fiefs, caused a major change in the structure of feudal armies.

The Indenture Contract System

In theory the feudal tenure system enabled a king to call on large bodies of cavalry and infantry, but in practice neither force could be relied on to any great extent. In England, for example, William the Conqueror distributed the land amongst his barons in such a manner as to provide between six and seven thousand knights. In 1277 Edward I summoned all the knights to his banner for a campaign against Wales: 375 answered the call. In 1346 Edward III was able to muster less than a thousand knights. In addition to this reluctance to answer the call to arms, the loyalties of the feudal host were usually divided between the bickering lords, making it almost impossible to manœuvre the army as a whole, and after forty days it was often impossible to hold the army together even if payment were offered. The levies were ill-trained, lacked any desire to fight and, outside of England, often owed no direct allegiance to the king. Furthermore the wars between England and France, mainly prolonged struggles for towns and castles, led to a need for well-equipped and trained foot soldiers, archers and engineers, who would remain in the field for long periods.

The main trouble lay in the fact that feudal armies had been organised to defend the realm, and were totally unsuitable for the offensive action required of them in subsequent centuries. Apart from the reluctance of the knights to leave their estates, the shire levy could not be forced to serve outside their own country. Although replacements for knights might be hired with the scutage money, there were still insufficient reliable infantrymen.

As early as the late eleventh century military leaders had recognised that no army could be supplied entirely by the feudal system and had begun to employ mercenaries, mainly crossbowmen and spearmen. By the middle of the twelfth century mercenaries formed a substantial part of most armies: Brabançon spearmen worked for France, Italy and England from the thirteenth until the early fourteenth centuries, when they were superseded by Gascon infantry and mounted crossbowmen. But the hiring of mercenaries was an expensive method of waging war, taking perhaps more than half the king's annual revenue, and the feudal army as such continued to be employed, stiffened by these mercenaries.

Edward I attempted to increase the number of his cavalry by making all landowners with estates worth more than £20 a year render the military service of a knight, but this move was resisted. Edward III ran into similar resistance when he tried to make communities pay for their contingents to the shire levy, hoping thus to raise a professional and well-equipped infantry force. Because of this resistance, during the period c. 1300–1340 the three Edwards of England began to develop a purely mercenary army. Mercenaries fought for England against the Welsh and Scots and the system was perfected during Edward III's campaigns against the French, when the English army was composed largely of paid men. Because the *Magna Carta* forbade the extensive use of foreign troops by a king of England, these mercenaries were for the most part Englishmen; in effect a small but professional army of paid volunteers. The men were selected by military leaders at village archery contests, the men competing for the honour of being chosen. This form of selective service was unknown elsewhere.

In 1341 Edward III revolutionised the whole structure of medieval armies by instituting a system of written indentured contracts between the Crown and prominent military leaders, a method of raising a professional army which spread to most of northern and western Europe, becoming standard practice by the late fourteenth century and remaining in use in England and France until the end of the Hundred Years War in 1453. Under this system the military leaders or 'captains' contracted with the king to provide an agreed number of men for military service, promising to bring them to a place of assembly by a certain date. The indenture set out precisely how long the men would have to serve (traditionally a minimum of forty days and a maximum of one year), their rates of pay, obligations and privileges. Such armed bands were usually of all arms; men-at-arms, mounted and foot archers and spearmen. The first instalment of their wages was normally paid by the commander of the band, the king giving securities to repay the money at the point of assembly or as soon after that date as possible. For the Agincourt campaign the Duke of Clarence provided 240 men-at-arms and 720 mounted archers, a weekly wages bill of over £250, so obviously the captains had to be men of wealth, or men capable of raising the necessary capital on the strength of their military experience.

The mercenaries themselves may be divided into three main groups. Firstly, the professional soldiers hired to fight for their own or a foreign country, usually for a particular campaign. Secondly, allies subsidised by another, with or without a feudal link. (For example, in 1100 Henry I of England bestowed on the Count of Flanders a money fief of £500 a year in return for the services of a thousand knights, and the Count of Brittany had a similar arrangement with the English king.) Thirdly, the household knights attending a lord. Many churchmen had such entourages, but household knights were chiefly cultivated by the various kings as a household cavalry, used in conjunction with the sergeants-at-arms, since they provided the king with a supply of loyal field and staff officers. (In the mid-thirteenth century Henry III of England had a small standing 'army' of about 100 household knights, 100 mounted sergeants and a rather larger number of infantry and archers, which formed the nucleus of any army he raised.)

In France the contract system, run on similar lines, was

known as *lettre de retinue*. France was faced with a greater problem than England, having to provide numerous small garrisons to protect castles and cities against English raiders, *and* put an army into the field. This was a major cause of the frequent and prolonged use of the *Arrière-ban* as an infantry force in the field, the levy being called out more often than in England, mostly for campaigns under the king.

The Condotta System

Because feudalism was based on a rural society it was especially ill-developed in northern Italy and Flanders, where the wealth and organisation of the cities founded in Roman times was often far greater than that of the lords. Indeed many nobles became heavily involved in trade and abandoned their country estates to live in the flourishing cities, thus giving those cities control of the surrounding countryside. Florence, Venice, Genoa and Pisa were such cities in northern Italy; Ypres, Ghent and Bruges in Flanders. These cities were independent and self-governing, symbols of liberty to the peasants, many of whom abandoned the manors for the cities. Fierce civic pride replaced homage to a lord, and each city ultimately came to regard its thriving neighbours as rivals, leading to wars amongst themselves for dominance. By the end of the thirteenth century the free cities, or *comuni*, of northern Italy had exhausted themselves with their internal fighting and gradually relinquished their independence to local *signori* such as the Estes of Ferrara, the Visconti of Milan, the Carraras of Padua, the Della Scalas of Verona, and the Gonzagas of Mantua.

Each of the *comuni* and small republics had its own militia to carry out police duties, garrison castles and guard the borders, but as the *signori* began in turn to struggle for dominance, each trying to seize his neighbour's territory, it became obvious that larger, more professional, armies were needed. Most *comuni* and republics raised troops from their own populations and some of these professional soldiers became famous, such as the crossbowmen of Genoa. However, by as early as 1310–1330 the *signori* had also begun to employ bands of foreign mercenaries in these internal wars, mostly from Germany. These bands were known as Compagnie di Ventura, companies of fortune, and usually consisted of between fifty and a hundred men, who reverted to brigandage at the end of their service. Some of these companies were the Compagnie della Colomba (Company of the Pigeon) which pillaged Umbria; the Compagnie della Ceruglio (the name of the commander) which plundered Tuscany; and the Compagnie della Siena which helped the Tolomei family in its bid to conquer Siena. The first company of Italians was the Compagnie di St Giorgio, commanded by Alberico da Barbiano, in the middle of the fourteenth century. The first really large band of mercenaries was also called the Company of St George, or the Great Company, led by Werner von Urslingen, known as Duke Guarnieri, and was composed of 6,000 Germans and Swiss. This company fought for various factions in Italy until 1351. An even larger but later company was the Grand Company of Fra Moriale, (he had been expelled from the Order of St John), which had 7,000 mounted men-at-arms and 2,000 crossbowmen.

The captains of these bands were often of noble blood and had personal fortunes, for they were obliged to guarantee their men's pay when the company was unemployed. Such an arrangement was called *Condotta*, from which came the term *Condottiero* for the commander. There were four types of pay under this system: 1. *Condotta a soldo disteso;* full pay while the commander held the company under the command of a lord. 2. *Condotta a mezzo soldo;* half pay while the company was unemployed. 3. *Condotta di aspetto* (waiting); the commander receiving a small payment in return for holding the company ready to fight when needed, which often became 4. *Raccomandigia*, when the commander received a larger payment for the company serving a lord in peacetime as a police force and border guard.

The Compagnie di Ventura were mostly mounted men-at-arms, with only a few crossbowmen and spearmen. The arrival of the Landsknechts and Swiss mercenaries towards the end of the fifteen century brought an end to the era of these companies.

The Free Companies

In the fourteenth century neither France nor England had the financial resources to engage in prolonged warfare yet the Hundred Years War did create large armies, attracting landless knights, younger sons and bastards of lords, and those seeking to gain a knighthood in the field, from all parts of Europe. These men, together with the ordinary foot soldiers, formed themselves into Free Companies after the *Condotta* style and hired out to the most generous side, seeking fame, fortune and perhaps land. However, because these Free Companies were independent of both England and France and had no means of making a living except by war, they were extremely difficult to disband when a campaign came to an end, and the men who hired them were forced to find fresh battles for them to fight in order to prevent a lapse into brigandage. Thus the Free Companies had an influential role in the wars of the fourteenth and fifteenth centuries. The Dukes of Anjou led successive armies of such companies into Italy in an attempt to win the kingdom of Naples. Edward III repeatedly invaded France in an effort to regain his inheritance. The Duke of Orleans used the companies to try to win a kingdom in the papal territories. The Duke of Lancaster spent a fortune on them while attempting to seize the crown of Castile. The Free Companies which took part in these local wars frequently remained in the area long after their leaders had abandoned their projects, so creating further problems.

After the French defeat at Poitiers in 1356 many of these

Free Companies resorted to brigandage as a means of making a living, usually establishing themselves in a stronghold from which they could terrorise the surrounding countryside into paying tribute, capturing for ransom any wealthy travellers who had the misfortune to pass through their area, and sometimes uniting with other armed bands to sack a poorly defended town. Soon the whole of southern France was overrun, together with much of Normandy and the frontiers of Brittany. In 1361 many of the French, English and German companies were employed by the Marquis of Montferrato to fight the lords of Milan, this being mainly a means of getting them out of France. Enguerrand de Coucy took a band called the Guglers through Burgundy into Switzerland, where they were defeated by the men of Berne. Sir John Hawkwood of Hedingham Sible in Essex, who had fought at Crécy and Poitiers, formed his White Company of 2,500 men-at-arms and 2,000 longbowmen after the Treaty of Bretigny in 1360 and subsequently fought in the Italian wars, first for Pisa against Florence, then for the Visconti against the Pope, and finally for Florence until his death in 1394. The Great Company went to Avignon and forced the Pope to pay them large sums of money before Bertrand du Guesclin, later Constable of France, led them across the Pyrenees in 1364 to help Henry, Count of Trastamara to gain the crown of Castile from his half brother Pedro the Cruel. The Black Prince took some English from Gascony and other Free Companies and marched into Castile in 1367 in support of Pedro and war waged in Castile for twenty years. All this had somewhat curbed the chaos in France, but bands continued to plunder Brittany and Normandy and fight over the borders of Languedoc, where 'English' companies could always be found to fight the troops of the king of France, until the end of the Hundred Years War.

Warfare in Spain

Warfare was somewhat different in Spain, the reconquest of the Iberian peninsula from the Moors in the twelfth and thirteenth centuries being a series of sporadic forays and skirmishes between light cavalry rather than 'set-piece' battles. Both sides conducted raids with plunder as the main objective and this type of guerilla warfare drove the population from the land to seek the protection of the walls of towns and castles. Therefore, in many ways Spain came to resemble Italy, with a number of powerful cities, each more or less self-sufficient but, unlike Italy, remaining under royal sovereignty. Perhaps the greatest of these cities was Barcelona, one of the great commercial and naval powers of the Mediterranean, rivalling Florence and Genoa.

Because of this method of development feudalism was never as strong in Spain as it was in England, France and Germany, although the kings and barons had feudal followings which, with the military orders, provided the bulk of the armies of medieval Spain. Once the Moors had been driven out the military orders and barons turned their attentions to each others' possessions and during the fourteenth and much of the fifteenth centuries Castile and Aragon were torn by civil wars. During these wars most of the independent cities raised a militia force for their own protection, and to supplement or rival the armies of the kings, barons and military orders, according to which side they chose to support at the time. In Castile these militias were known as *Hermandades*, in Aragon as *Comunidades*.

In the late fifteenth century the reconquest of Granada was achieved, due to the united energies of Ferdinand of Aragon and Isabella of Castile. This Reconquista lasted from 1481 until 1491 and was accomplished by armies containing large numbers of feudal levies, but backed by Swiss mercenaries, German and Italian artillery specialists, volunteers from England, France and Germany, and the *Santa Hermandad*, a federation of the police forces originally raised by the independent cities for their own protection, but now converted into the beginnings of a national army, paid for by the Crown, by a tax on the clergy and nobility as well as the burghers, and under the control of a royal officer.

The French National Army

The French victories over the English in the 1430s led to the Truce of Tours in 1444 which lasted until 1449. Charles VII of France used this lull to reorganise his forces into a national army. In 1439 under the *Ordonnance sur la Gendarmerie* he had made the first steps towards such an army, led by royal officers and financed by a royal tax, and at the same time forbade his nobles to raise troops without royal licence. This provoked a rising amongst the nobles, which was crushed, leaving the way clear for France to become the first European nation to have a standing army.

Charles' aim was to form a police force to suppress the Free Companies and provide a nucleus for an army to defeat England. Amnesties were granted to the less villainous Free Companies and under the Constable de Richemont and the Comte de Dunois fifteen *Compagnies d'Ordonnance du Roi* were formed by 1445, each commanded by a nobleman chosen for his skill and loyalty, the company being known by the name of its commander. These companies, later increased to twenty, formed the king's cavalry and were kept under strict control, lodged in selected towns and paid for by the provinces.

In 1448 another ordinance was passed which created the Franc-archiers, an infantry militia. Each group of fifty hearths in France had to provide, equip and pay one archer or crossbowman, and by this ordinance Charles created a permanent force of 8,000 infantry. In time of war the king paid for these men. During the same period the Royal Artillery was organised and trained by Gasper and Jean Bureau until it was the most technically advanced and effective artillery in Europe.

In the last campaigns of the Hundred Years War the infantry, cavalry and artillery of the Royal Army of France were triumphant time after time, defeating the English in the field and recapturing castles and towns in rapid succession. At the close of the war in 1453 France had a regular army of at least 12,000 men-at-arms and crossbowmen, supplemented for the invasion of Italy at the end of the century by Swiss, German and Gascon mercenaries. The other major nations soon followed this example, with the exception of England, where it was to be another two centuries before a proper standing army was formed.

The Livery and Maintenance System

By the end of the Hundred Years War England was in chaos with the people in rebellion against the heavy taxes for the war, the great barons settling their quarrels with private wars, and the rivalry between the Houses of York and Lancaster leading inexorably to the Wars of the Roses. Many English soldiers returning from France found employment in the private armies of the barons, and the king, lacking a standing army, was able to control disloyal barons only by using the armies of those barons who remained loyal. This weakness in the royal authority led to corruption in the courts of law, for whenever the interests of a landowner were involved in a legal case rival bodies of armed men, wearing the liveries of the lords who maintained them, would ride into the county town and intimidate judge and jury.

Since justice was no longer obtainable, many of the yeomen and lesser gentry also turned to the barons for protection. These yeomen and gentry entered into a contract known as Livery and Maintenance, whereby they undertook to wear the baron's livery, i.e. a tunic in his colours and bearing his badge, and fight for him in times of need. In return they received his protection whenever they needed it. These large private armies, and contract troops raised by the Crown, formed the bulk of the armies involved in the Wars of the Roses, 1455–1485. The royal or feudal levy was only called out at moments of great need, almost all the fighting being between the nobility and their retainers, and because of this the social progress of the country suffered little. However, this situation was responsible for Henry VII having, at the end of the wars, a national 'army' consisting of only a few hundred Yeomen of the Guard, the household cavalry, the gunners at various royal castles, and the small garrison at Calais, whereas most other monarchs now had substantial standing armies.

The 'People's Armies' of Switzerland and Bohemia

Another type of army to emerge during the fourteenth and fifteenth centuries was the 'people's army'. In 1291 the three Forest Cantons of Uri, Schwyz and Unterwalden united against the barons of Austria and Bavaria to begin the war of liberation which was to last until 1499. These three cantons were later joined by others to form a confederation of peoples who spoke different languages, had different religions, and came from different races, yet who were able to weld themselves into one nation capable of defeating Europe's chivalry with peasant foot soldiers and governing themselves without the assistance of nobles or a king. These foot soldiers, the Swiss pikemen, began hiring themselves out to other European nations after defeating Charles the Bold at Nancy in 1477, and became the élite infantry of Europe until made obsolete by the arquebus.

In Bohemia at the beginning of the fifteenth century John Hus set himself the task of attacking corruption in the Bohemian church. He was burnt at the stake in 1415, seized upon as a martyr by the Bohemians, who wished to break from the Holy Roman Empire to form an independent nation, and so precipitated the Hussite Wars, 1419–1478.

At this time the Bohemian nobles could be counted by the score, while the German chivalry was numbered in thousands. The Bohemian peasants and burghers were poorly armed and undisciplined. The task of forging a national army from this unlikely material fell to Jan Ziska, who had acquired military experience fighting with the Poles against the Teutonic knights. Ziska was a natural leader and a great general. Under his rigid discipline the entire adult male population of Bohemia was conscripted for military service, enabling large armies to be fielded by a comparatively small state. Whilst half this army fought, the other half cultivated the land, roles being reversed periodically.

Ziska was the first European commander to make full use of artillery and see the value of a laager of wagons for cancelling the threat of a cavalry charge and steadying a peasant army. He organised a special corps of wagoners which was continually drilled until it could form circle, square or triangle within minutes. Men armed with pikes and flails blocked the gaps between the wagons, and from the wagons themselves other men discharged missiles at the enemy.

This army, which marched into action behind a sacred chalice, roaring the Ziska psalm, was gradually weakened during the Hussite Wars, losses being replaced by soldiers of fortune.

The Landsknechts

In the last quarter of the fifteenth century one other body of men rose to prominence; the Landsknechts. It is believed the first company may have been raised in the province of Brisgau as early as 1474, organised and armed in somewhat the same manner as the Swiss pikemen but using shorter pikes. At first just a band of mercenary adventurers, willing to fight for anyone for pay, in 1486 Maximilian I eliminated the more dubious members and raised the Landsknechts to the status of a disciplined standing army, encouraging knights to serve in their ranks and nobles to lead them. The

Landsknechts were superior to all other infantry, with the exception of the Swiss, who defeated the Landsknechts repeatedly until the sixteenth century.

Cavalry Organisation

The smallest unit within the medieval cavalry was the knight and his personal retainers, known collectively throughout western Europe as a 'lance', not to be confused with a retinue, which also contained foot soldiers and was usually split up at the assembly point. The English lance theoretically consisted of a knight, a man-at-arms and two mounted archers, (Chaucer writing c.1360 lists a knight, a squire and a mounted archer), but the French 'lance garnis' of 1450 contained a total of five men; a man-at-arms, a squire and three mounted archers, or two mounted archers and a light cavalryman or hobilar. In Italy the earliest unit mentioned for the Compagnie di Ventura is a *barbuta* of a mounted sergeant and a man-at-arms. This was changed in the 1350s to a lance of a corporal, a squire and a boy. The Knights Templar each had two squires in attendance on the battlefield, one to hold the knight's shield and lance, the other in charge of the spare horse or horses at the rear.

In Italy five lances made a *posta* and five *poste* a *bandiera* (flag), i.e. a unit of twenty-five heavy cavalry. According to a Royal Ordonnance of 1351 the French cavalry was grouped in 'squadrons' (*routes*) of a definite number and a strict system of muster and review by royal officers ensured they were always at full strength and properly armed and mounted. No number is quoted for the squadron, but in England such squadrons varied from 25 to 80 in number, giving an average of about 50, and were commanded by a knight flying a pennoncelle on his lance. The Latin term for this commander was *Vintenaires*, suggesting twenty may have been the original number for a squadron.

Several such squadrons, perhaps totalling two or three hundred men, formed the equivalent of a modern regiment or Byzantine *banda* of 450 men, (Byzantine military methods were widely studied in western Europe), and were led by a knight bachelor, entitled to fly a pennon. Several of these 'regiments' were united under the command of their tenant-in-chief – a baron, earl, duke or prince – who flew a banner. The Latin names for commanders of such units were *centenaries* and *millenaries*. At Bannockburn in 1314 the 3,000 English cavalrymen were divided into ten Battles, each of 300 men. These were then formed into three lines of three Battles, each under an overall commander. The tenth Battle formed an advanced guard.

From the 1350s the command of a Battle was also given to knights below the rank of peer who had valuable military experience or who could bring to the field of battle a great number of fighting men. These commanders were known as knights banneret, often standing in for tenants-in-chief who had no real qualification to play the part of a military leader. Such men were du Guesclin, who came from an obscure Breton family, and Sir John Hawkwood, who is said to have been the son of a tanner. Indeed many of the most famous English captains of the Hundred Years War were well below baronial rank: Sir Thomas Dagworth, Sir John Chandos, Sir Hugh Calveley, Sir Walter Manny and Sir Robert Knollys – *Robert le Terrible* to the French – who served in France from 1356 to 1376 as captain of one of Edward III's Free Companies.

Cavalry 'constabularies' are also recorded, but their size is unknown. Constables were often appointed to command the tenants of churchmen, unless the bishop or abbot was also a fighting man: in 1369 Edward III summoned both laymen and clerics to take up arms against a French invasion and as late as 1513, on Flodden Field, a Scottish archbishop was slain in battle.

The cavalry consisted therefore of knights, sergeants and men-at-arms and it is as well at this point to define precisely what these terms mean. The nobles and knights were of various ranks, by which they may be positively identified: barons, earls, dukes and princes in the peerage; and knights banneret, knights bachelor and simple knights. These men were the officers of the army, with the household knights and the poorer knights, who lacked a retinue, fighting in the ranks. They and their horses were heavily armoured. The sergeants were all those below the rank of knight who had the equipment of a knight, or a lighter form of it. Their horses were smaller than those of the knights and were unarmoured. The term man-at-arms actually applies to all mounted fighting men who wore armour, but although a knight might therefore be called a man-at-arms, a man-at-arms was not necessarily a knight, being possibly a sergeant or a squire. Thus the sergeants and squires, who normally fought in the ranks behind the first rank of knights and peers, formed the bulk – the rank and file – of the cavalry.

The position of the squire on the field of battle needs some explanation. Young boys of the knightly class were sent as pages to the castle of their father's liege lord at about the age of seven, graduating to the rank of squire when they were about thirteen or fourteen. As squires they were apprentice knights and were trained in the knightly pursuits until about the age of twenty or twenty one, when they were knighted. The senior squire – the one most eligible for knighthood – was known as the squire of the body and he accompanied his lord in battle, having a number of responsibilities: to assist the knight in donning his armour; hand him fresh weapons to replace lost or broken ones; catch his horse if the lord was dismounted, or supply a replacement if the horse was wounded or killed; take charge of any prisoners captured by the lord; rescue the lord if he was taken prisoner; carry him from the field if wounded; lend his assistance if his lord was attacked by several men at once; act as subaltern to the retinue.

We tend to think of these squires as gay, gallant youths, but the medieval manuscripts portray them as mature men of a rather heavy type – knights in all but name. (The gay, bright 'squire' of romances is probably the page, or varlet, who carried the lord's helmet.) The squires are usually portrayed bare headed or hooded, and unarmed – in the tenth and eleventh centuries squires were actually forbidden to wear a hauberk or helmet and were allowed to use only a light lance. There are few portraits of squires, but those few show them either unarmoured or wearing a thick quilted gambeson for protection. From this it may be seen that the squire was roughly equal to a sergeant as a fighting man, both forming a medium cavalry to boost the relatively few heavy cavalry.

The 'light cavalry' was represented by the hobilars, a term applied to unarmoured spearmen or archers mounted on the same type of horse as the sergeant and squire. They were used as despatch riders and scouts and normally played no part in the cavalry fighting. The mounted archers re-ferred to earlier were not cavalry in the true sense, being more akin to mounted infantry, using their horses only to get them to the scene of action, although they were some-times used as light cavalry to pursue a defeated enemy. Edward III created his mounted archer corps in 1334 in order to obtain greater mobility in his border wars with Scotland. The use of large numbers of archers supported by men-at-arms made it essential that the two arms should be able to travel at the same speed, and therefore during the Hundred Years War an increasing proportion of English archers was mounted on cheap nags, and by the second half of the fourteenth century some French infantry were also mounted, presumably so that they might overtake and engage the highly mobile 'flying columns' of the English raids.

Eustach Deschamps, writing in 1360, states that there were three types of war horse: the great destrier, which was tall and heavy (though not like a modern cart horse) and was in fact used only for the joust; the lighter and faster courser, about $14\frac{1}{2}$ to 15 hands high and resembling a modern heavy hunter or large show jumper; and the rounsey, a poor breed of horse used for labouring tasks. In fact all troops rode the rounsey, the knights alone having coursers, led by the squires, which they mounted as battle became imminent. (At Bannockburn King Robert of Scotland was still seated on his rounsey, armed only with an axe, when attacked suddenly by Sir Henry Bohun. He knocked Bohun's lance aside with his axe and as the Englishman swept past brained him with a second blow to the back of the helmet.)

Infantry Organisation

Contrary to popular belief the infantry of the medieval period were not *all* an inferior rabble used only for carrying out menial tasks in camp. Admittedly the levies were frequently so poorly armed and ill trained that they stood no chance at all against a cavalry charge, but most armies had a hard core of mercenaries, usually spearmen and crossbowmen, who worked in conjunction with the cavalry and formed a vital part of the army (see Chapter Four).

The French professional infantry of the middle of the fourteenth century consisted of spearmen and crossbowmen, organised in companies of 25 to 30 men, each company commanded by a constable who flew a pennoncelle on his lance. Crossbowmen had been engaged since the twelfth century in all parts of Europe. The best companies came from Genoa and from the Low Countries – Holland, Hainault and Brabant – and were often called *routiers*, meaning highwaymen, for they usually resorted to brigandage if unemployed. (The Compagnie d'Ordonnance of the mid-fifteenth century had 500 men, 100 lances of five men, as listed above. All were mounted.)

In the English armies infantry were also commanded by constables on occasions, these constables being tenants of the

Crown who held their land in return for such service. At the end of the twelfth century a 'constabulary' of Welsh infantry numbered 500, and this seems to have been a uniform size for infantry units of that time. (When the English army crossed the Somme prior to the battle of Agincourt in 1415, the advanced guard consisted of 500 men-at-arms.) The longbowmen were organised in companies drawn from the parish areas, under the command of a Master Bowman. The companies allocated to each of the three Battles of the army were placed under the overall command of a knight or sergeant. During the reign of Edward III (1327–1376) a corps of archers numbering 120 was formed from the best bowmen in the kingdom, and these were called the Archers of the King's Guard, forming an élite body of troops round the king with the sergeants-at-arms and the household cavalry. The French copied this idea in the second half of the century, raising a corps of Scottish archers known as the Scottish Archers of the Guard. The English Archers of the Guard were apparently perpetuated by Henry VII when in 1485 he formed the Yeomen of the Guard, a bodyguard of fifty archers under a captain. The guard was soon increased to 200 and by 1490 numbered 600. These archers were also armed with a halberd.

The Swiss phalanx of pikemen was also formed of disciplined companies, made up of men from each canton, a small division of territory similar to the English parish. These companies were grouped into three columns, the number of men in each varying according to the strength of the army: in the early days only four to five hundred, later from five to six thousand or more. The columns did not have an overall commander because the men of one canton would not serve under a citizen of another. A council of war, consisting of a captain from each canton, decided by majority vote who would command each column for the coming battle.

Ziska's Hussite army was organised with a wagon as the basic unit. Each wagon and its driver was accompanied by twenty men, half of them missile men, the other half armed with pikes and flails.

The Landsknechts were organised in companies of about 400 men, and these companies were usually grouped in three columns like the Swiss. The Spanish infantry of the late fifteenth century was divided into 'colonelcies', each consisting of a thousand men divided into four companies; one armed with sword and buckler, one with the pike, one with the arquebus, and the fourth as light horse, *ginetes*.

It may be seen from the above that the armies of this period employed a wide variety of troops or 'arms': heavy cavalry composed of peers and knights; medium cavalry of sergeants and squires; light cavalry or hobilars; heavy infantry in the form of dismounted men-at-arms; medium infantry of partially armoured professional crossbowmen and spearmen, other mercenaries such as the Scots Lowlanders fighting for France, and some of the better equipped city militias or shire levies; light infantry consisting of longbowmen, bowmen and unarmoured spearmen, especially the Welsh and Irish; and a 'rabble' consisting of peasantry armed with a variety of crude weapons.

The proportions of each of these arms varied from army to army and century to century. Edward I's army in Flanders at the end of the 13th century consisted of 895 cavalry, of whom 140 were peers and knights, and about 7,810 infantry, three-quarters of them Welsh. At Falkirk in 1298 he had 2,500 cavalry, 10,000 Welsh bowmen and spearmen, and 2,500 bowmen of Cheshire and Lancashire against Wallace's 200 cavalry and 10,000 infantry, which included several thousand archers. At Crécy the proportion was about 1,150 men-at-arms and 2,745 mounted infantry or hobilars, to 5,500 Welsh and English longbowmen and 1,750 Welsh spearmen. Ten years later at Poitiers there were 3,000 men-at-arms, 2,000 archers (about half of them mounted) and 1,000 'sergeants' (hobilars?), but at the battle of Agincourt Henry V employed no less than 5,000 archers to 1,000 men-at-arms. Edward IV's force which landed at

Calais in 1475, together with the forces of the Dukes of
Burgundy and Brittany, had 1,500 men-at-arms, 15,000
mounted archers, plus foot soldiers and artillery. The French
armies usually consisted of up to fifty per cent peasant
levies, the remainder being almost all men-at-arms, with
between 3,000 and 5,000 hired crossbowmen. The vast
Spanish army raised in 1483 to drive the Moors out of
Granada consisted of about 12,000 light and heavy cavalry
to about 30,000 infantry, with an unknown number of
gunners, miners, pioneers and foragers to a total of perhaps
80,000 men. In all these cases the nobles and knights formed
only a hard core of the army, the bulk being sergeants and
squires and mounted or unmounted soldiers. On average an
army of between ten and fifteen thousand men, a large army
for that time, would have perhaps 200 knights, this being
considered a strong force of chivalry.

The Swiss frequently deployed up to a quarter of their
army in crossbowmen, used as skirmishers, and never less
than one tenth. At Morat in 1476, 10,000 out of 35,000 were
light troops, but this was an exceptional case.

Army Formations

It was usual to divide an army into three divisions, called
Battles, with the light troops occasionally operating
separately under their own commander. The three Battles
are generally referred to as the Vanguard (Vaward Battle in
England, Avant Garde in France), the Main Battle and the
Rearward Battle. The three Battles always marched in this
order and normally deployed for battle with the Main
Battle, the most honourable command and usually led by
the king or his deputy, in the centre; the Vanguard on the
right as the second most honourable command; and the
Rearward Battle on the left. Where there was insufficient
room for such deployment the Battles might be placed with
two in the front line and one in reserve, or in three successive lines. The Rearward Battle should not be confused with

a rearguard, which would be a force specially selected to protect the rear of a retreating force, for command of a rearguard was considered a great honour. Each Battle would be broken up into many smaller units as outlined earlier, each retinue under its lord, or an allocated commander if the retinues were grouped by arms, as they usually were.

The Bohemian army of the Hussite Wars always moved in five parallel columns with the cavalry and artillery in the centre, flanked on either side by two columns of wagons with their infantry. The Swiss operated in the orthodox three Battles or phalanxes, called *vorhut*, *gewaltshaufen* and *nachhut*, but usually advanced in echelon, that is the right hand column leading, the centre one a little way back to its left and the left hand column a little behind and left of centre.

The two principal officers of royal armies, next to the king and his sons, were the Marshal and Constable. The Constable of France led the Vanguard of the Royal Army during the thirteenth century and by the fourteenth had risen to become its commander-in-chief. The rank of Marshal was subordinate to that of Constable, except in England. Deputies of the Marshal preceded the army on its march to select camp sites and allocate sectors of the site for each noble's pavilion.

Logistics

In addition to the fighting men there were always many non-combatants with an army. These included women to cook and wash for the men, pages, grooms, musicians, legal and clerical staffs, quartermasters, carpenters, farriers, saddlers, armourers, bowyers, fletchers, wheelwrights, carters, smiths, tentmakers and painters. At Agincourt the headquarters of Henry V contained, amongst others, 15 musicians, 16 clergy, 60 grooms, 86 yeomen, 120 labourers, 124 carpenters, 20 surgeons, 120 miners and 75 gunners.

Having raised an army, the king had to transport, feed and pay it. The evidence available seems to indicate that the logistics of war were fully understood and were dealt with in much the same way as staffs dealt with logistic problems up to the utilisation of railways for warlike purposes. The men were obliged to arrive at the muster point with their own arms, armour and horses, and by and large medieval armies solved the provisions problem by living off the land, although English armies invading France usually took a small amount of food with them to allow the army to become established across the channel. However, stocks of arrows, bow staves, bow cords, feathers, guns, gunpowder, horseshoes, pontoons and wagons had to be purchased and gathered at one place, and in the case of an English army invading France a vast number of transports had to be accumulated. The transportation and feeding of horses was a particular problem for the English kings. A duke was entitled to take fifty horses, an earl twenty-four, a knight six, a squire four, and a horse archer one. Added to these were the pack animals and horses of the wagons and trades-men. Henry V is estimated to have shipped 25,000 horses to France for the Agincourt campaign.

The speed at which an army could travel overland was greatly restricted by the wagons and the lack of roads. Frequently a breakdown in one wagon could delay the entire army. There were no accurate maps to assist in planning a campaign and knowledge of the surrounding countryside, and of the enemy's movements, was supplied by scouts, local informers and deserters. It was not unusual for armies to fail to locate each other and this was one of the main reasons why commanders frequently sent heralds to find the enemy with orders to offer battle at a particular place on a set day.

Until the middle of the fourteenth century armies were relatively simple in structure and organisation and the troops were paid by the king, who often relied on successful looting to pay the costs. However, by the fifteenth century

Fifteenth century camp with baggage wagons, kitchens, amusement booths and camp followers. A log forms the portcullis and the camp is fortified by what appear to be wooden shields on wheels.

armies were equipped with large siege trains of artillery and troops of engineers, and the bill was to a large extent paid by taxation. Rates of pay per day in the English army between 1316 and 1415 were: dukes 13s. 4d.; earls 6s. 8d.; barons and knights banneret 4s.; knights 2s.; constables, centenaries, sergeants and squires 1s.; mounted archers, armoured infantry, hobilars and vintenaries 6d.; vintenaries of the Welsh 4d.; foot archers 3d.; Welsh spearmen 2d.

All this made war an expensive business and for the Agincourt campaign Henry V had loans of £44,243 from the Church, £32,000 from the City of London, £9,000 from the religious orders, together with his own funds and many smaller loans, yet was forced to break up one of his crowns and distribute pieces of this and all the other crown jewels as securities to the various captains who had raised companies for the campaign.

CHAPTER TWO

Armour

UNTIL the end of the thirteenth century the armour and weapons of Europe had changed little from those used in Viking times, but at the turn of the century there began an era of new, more powerful infantry weapons capable of penetrating the mail shirt, which had until then proved an adequate defence against any weapon. The new weapons caused the armourers to devise more and more complex systems of defence, until the advent of an efficient arquebus in the sixteenth century rendered armour obsolete and changed the whole concept of war. The period 1300 to 1500 is therefore one of considerable importance in the development of armour.

Mail

Mail was made of thousands of interlinked rings, generally of wire with the ends flattened and punched to receive a rivet, although some were punched out of sheet metal. These rings were so closely knitted that it was impossible to get a dagger point between them. Mail was flexible but

Short-sleeved German mail shirt, 1425–1450.

had several serious disadvantages. The links could be broken by a violent thrust or cut, the broken links being driven into the wound and turning it septic. Thicker rings gave greater strength but at the cost of flexibility. Thickly padded garments were therefore worn under the mail to support it but even this combination could not prevent severe bruising and even the breaking of bones by heavy buffets with a sword or axe. Other disadvantages were that the mail was heavy, about thirty pounds, with most of that weight hanging on the shoulders, and the elbows and knees could not be bent without some chafing.

Another form of armour was scale, usually consisting of small rectangular plates of horn or sometimes metal attached to a linen or leather garment. This was fairly common until the thirteenth century, and remained in service amongst the infantry into the first half of the fourteenth century, being lighter and more flexible than mail.

By 1300 the mail shirt, or hauberk, covered the body, extending down the arms to end in bag mittens – a slit being left under the wrist to enable the hand to be withdrawn, a mail coif protected the head, and mail hose guarded the legs, but by now most mounted men had pieces of plate armour at the elbows, knees, shins and hands, with quilted covering on the thighs. This mixture of mail, plate and quilted armour is characteristic of the first half of the fourteenth century.

Early Plate Armour

The first plate defences were those for knee and thigh, which were particularly vulnerable to the weapons of the infantry, and the point where most chafing would occur for mounted men, although this seems to have been a secondary consideration since some of these reinforcements were merely strapped over the mail. In other cases the mail hose was cut and fastened above and below the knee with tapes, and a saucer-shaped plate of iron, called a poleyn, fitted over the knee cap. This development took place about 1225. By 1250–1260 a triangular extension had been added to protect the outside of the knee joint and a narrow plate extended down the front of the shin, tapering to a point. These defences were strapped on at knee and mid-calf.

The weakest point in a mounted man's armour was still his legs and by the last quarter of the thirteenth century two separate tubes of quilted armour were being worn on the thighs, over the mail hose. These were called cuisses and were sometimes reinforced by long strips of metal, only the heads of the securing rivets being visible on the outside. In Germany the cuisses frequently extended over the knee in place of the poleyn, being laced below the knee.

During the period 1300–1330 these defences were improved, the cuisses often consisting of small plates riveted to a fabric (the old scale armour), the lower leg being more fully protected by greaves, which were in two halves, hinged down the outside and buckled on the inside, with the lower edge shaped to fit over the instep and ankle bones. At the same time the extension on the outside of the poleyn was enlarged into a fan shape, and the poleyn and greave were riveted together with a deep plate below the poleyn overlapping the top of the greave. The feet were now protected by sabatons, small overlapping plates or lames, riveted to a fabric. The prick spur, a single spike on a U-shaped arm which strapped round the foot, was replaced c. 1330 by the rowel spur, a spiked disc. At first the rowel and the U-arm were separated by a long bar but gradually this bar was shortened until the rowel was close to the heel.

During the middle of the century the quilted cuisse was replaced by a large plate curving well round the outside of the thigh, although in Germany mail still remained the most popular form of leg defence. Further protection was given by an extra plate running the length of the cuisse and hinged to its outer edge. By about 1370 plate cuisses were common throughout most of Europe and therefore by that date the leg was completely protected by plate armour.

Plate reinforcement for the elbow was introduced c. 1260 and was worn by most knights by 1300. This consisted initially of a cup-shaped defence, called the couter, strapped over the elbow, but by the 1320s long plates curving half round the forearm and upper arm had been added, called the vambrace and rerebrace respectively. Another curved plate, the spaudler, was sometimes attached to the shoulder of the hauberk. This was soon divided into several strips or lames

Pair of Milanese gauntlets, finger plates missing, *c*. 1380–1400.

to give greater freedom of movement. Circular plates called besagues were often laced to the outside of the elbow and the front of the shoulder to protect the joints in the same way that the poleyn had been extended. By the 1350s such arm defences were in common use throughout northern and western Europe, although on the Continent the lower arm was frequently protected only by the hauberk and padded liner, or with the plate under the mail. In Italy in particular the use of plate armour on arms was slow in developing and even in the second half of the century it was common for the arm to be protected by only a short sleeved hauberk and the quilted liner extending to the wrist. This method had its disadvantages but undoubtedly gave greater freedom to the sword arm.

About 1296 the bag mittens began to be replaced by gauntlets of small overlapping plates riveted to a leather glove. Some of these gauntlets had quite large cuffs of plates and by 1350 this had developed into a large flared cuff formed from a single plate. The knuckles were sometimes armed with short spikes called gadlings.

Ailettes

About 1270 there appeared another 'reinforcement' called the ailette, which was strapped or laced to the point of the shoulder and appears to have been designed to prevent a sword cut to the side of the neck. They were most frequently made of parchment or leather and it is doubtful if they had any real functional role, it being more probable that they were purely decorative, since they bore the wearer's heraldic insignia. Ailettes were usually rectangular but occasionally round, diamond, or even cross-shaped and reached a peak of popularity in the first quarter of the fourteenth century. Thereafter their use declined and they do not appear much after 1350.

Early 14th Century Shields

By 1270 the long kite shield of the Normans was reduced to the shorter style known as the heater shield, although the truncated kite shield continued to be used by infantry in Italy until the fifteenth century. Few shields have survived from this era but a heater shield of c. 1330–1350 was made of wood 15 mm. thick, covered with parchment on both sides and with neck- and arm-straps and a pad for the fist. The shield was curved into a semi-cylindrical shape to give better protection and was about 95 cm. long. By the early fourteenth century the shield was flatter and hung by the neck-strap – the guige – until the lance was broken or discarded, when the rein hand was transferred to the straps (brases) on the back.

A small round buckler, held by a central grip behind the boss, was used by many foot soldiers. The shield was between ten and twelve inches in diameter, sometimes with a steel spike on the boss, and was usually hung on the belt at the left side, leaving both hands free for men such as archers until hand-to-hand fighting began. The buckler was held at arm's length when used for parrying. Infantry, and occasionally some knights, also used a round or oval targe of wood and iron between twenty-four and thirty inches in length. On rare occasions these had a horizontal slit for vision in the upper half and a vertical slit at the bottom right for the passage of a thrusting sword when locked in close mêlée. Crossbowmen were protected by spearmen or special pavisers, both of whom carried a large rectangular shield called a pavise, constructed of wickerwork or of wood covered with hide.

Early 14th Century Helmets

The fourteenth century was also a period of great change for helmets, although the simple, conical helmet with a nasal bar to protect the face, worn in the eleventh century by both infantry and cavalry, persisted until as late as *c.* 1400. Another type to continue in use was the early thirteenth century kettle hat or *chapel de fer*, which had a conical crown and a wide brim. This was worn by both foot soldiers and mounted men right through the 1300–1500 period, being both strong and light. Both these types of helmets were worn over the mail coif, which had a quilted arming cap beneath it consisting of a padded roll round the head and a very broad chin-strap to prevent chafing to the cheeks. However, by about 1296 two other pieces of plate armour were introduced to be worn in conjunction with the kettle hat in place of the coif. These were called the bevor and gorget and consisted of a high collar, the bevor, which extended up to the nose so that it covered the lower half of the face, and the gorget, which covered the throat and went down to the chest and shoulders.

The great helm of the thirteenth century was also used in the early fourteenth century, by this date having a conical top and reaching down to the shoulders, on which it rested, a point at the front extending on to the chest. However, by the end of the first quarter of the century the helm had become too heavy for continual wear in battle and was used only in tournaments, although a version called the barbuta, with a T-shaped face opening in the classical Corinthian style, came into use in Italy at the beginning of the fifteenth century and remained in use until *c.* 1470, the face opening having become larger as time went on.

For some time knights had been wearing a simple, globular steel cap called a cervelliere under their coif, placing their helm over their heads only at the moment of action. At the beginning of the fourteenth century this cap, or bascinet as it came to be called because of its shape, began to be used on its own, over the coif, and was soon improved by making the crown pointed to deflect blows, and extending the sides and back to protect the cheeks and the base of the neck. The globular style remained popular in France and Italy during the fourteenth century. By the 1320s a short mail 'curtain' called the aventail had been fitted to the rim of the bascinet and hung over the shoulders to protect the neck. At first this was attached to the inside of the helmet but later on staples were riveted round the edge of the bascinet, rings inserted in the upper edge of the aventail, and the two jointed by a cord threaded through them. Occasionally the lower edge of the aventail was also laced to the surcoat. In Italy the bascinet was frequently used without the aventail. The bascinet and the kettle hat were the two most common forms of helmet in the first half of the fourteenth century.

Early Body Armour

In the same period several different kinds of armour were used to supplement the hauberk. As we have seen, the hauberk was already reinforced by a padded liner, the correct name for which is hacqueton or aketon. This was a shirt-like garment made of buckram, stuffed with cotton and stitched longitudinally, forming a stiff but not clumsy padding which ended at the knees. The sleeves were long and close fitting and there was a stiff, high standing collar to protect the neck. Another padded garment had been worn *over* the hauberk since the end of the twelfth century and this was called the gambeson. This also consisted of two thicknesses of coarse linen, stuffed with flax or rags and quilted to keep the stuffing in place. The gambeson reached only to the groin, had short wide sleeves or was sleeveless, and a wide stiff collar, perhaps lined with metal. Sometimes an abbreviated form was worn which resembled a small, stiff waistcoat.

During the first half of the fourteenth century infantrymen wore either the aketon or gambeson as body armour, or another form called a jack, a rough canvas or leather garment with metal or horn plates stitched inside it and laced down the front with an overlapping strip to protect the lacing. The poor knights, sergeants and squires also used these textile and leather body armours, all of which are frequently referred to in contemporary sources as 'pourpoint'. This has led to some confusion as to the different roles played by each type, and it is believed that the aketon and gambeson were originally the same garment, merely a padded liner, but that a difference developed between them later as more body armour became necessary.

About 1320 the hauberk was shortened, with cutaway sides, and a stiffened collar called a pixaine was added. The exact nature of this collar is not known but it appears to have been a separate collar of mail, made of thicker links to give greater rigidity. This form of hauberk was known as the lesser hauberk or haubergeon and was worn by foot soldiers as well as by mounted men, those worn by infantry usually having short sleeves.

As early as *c.* 1225 some other form of body armour was also being worn over the hauberk for greater protection. Contemporary sources refer to this as leather or iron plastrons, and it is known that even in Saxon times some form of breastplate was being worn *under* the hauberk, but the first illustrations of this armour do not occur until mid-century. At this period, and until about 1325, a long, loose, sleeveless gown known as the surcoat was worn over all else and this prevents a clear view of the extra body armour. Effigies of the mid-thirteenth century indicate that at this date the armour was short and usually sleeveless, apparently put over the head like a poncho with broad flaps extending under the arms from the front and buckling together down the middle of the back, or lacing up the sides. The garment is shown powdered with small dots, circles or flowers. By the 1280s illustrations occur which show that this powdering was in fact the heads of rivets attaching to the fabric vertical rows of narrow rectangular plates. The rows did not overlap but had a small space between them. These garments ended at the waist behind, but in the front hung down to mid-thigh, the part below the waist not being reinforced with metal. Four circular iron plates were often added to the exterior of the breast section for extra strength. The ordinary surcoat seems also to have been used for the attachment of reinforcing plates, for in the late thirteenth century many of these loose-fitting gowns are portrayed hanging stiffly from the point of the shoulder as if backed by some solid material.

By 1300 this had developed into the garment called the coat of plates, or pairs of plates. Because leather hardened in boiling wax (*cuir bouilli*) seems to have been more prevalent than iron at this time the garment is often referred to as the cuirie, or *paires de cuiraces*. This remained the most common type of body armour for mounted men, worn over the haubergeon, until the 1340s.

The surcoat itself was shortened at the front to mid-thigh length about 1325, the edge often being scalloped. Before this date the ends of the front 'tails' had often been tucked through the belt to give greater freedom of movement when on foot, and some examples appear to have been cut back at an angle. The rear tails were cut off to the same length about 1340, and this shortened version is referred to as the cyclas coat. The surcoat had been fastened at the waist by a silk cord: the cyclas was secured by a thin belt.

Fourteenth Century Equipments

So by about 1340–1350 the well equipped mounted man was wearing on his legs sabatons with rowel spurs, greaves, poleyns and cuisses, all worn over mail hose. On his body he placed an aketon, followed by a haubergeon, then a gambeson or a coat of plates and a surcoat or cyclas. His arms were protected by the sleeves of the haubergeon, with besagues at armpit and elbow, reinforced by plate on the upper and lower arm, the couter at the elbow, and the spaudler at the shoulder. On his hands were gauntlets of leather covered with plate. The aventail overlapped the shoulder defences and protected the neck, linking up with the bascinet. A kettle hat and bevor might be worn instead of the bascinet and aventail.

The spearmen of this period are described as wearing short mail coats, light helmets and carrying targes. Archers and other light troops usually favoured a light quilted body armour and the simple cervelliere, though some had a coat of plates called a brigandine, which seems to have been similar to the jack but more expensive, being made of smaller plates to give greater flexibility. Crossbowmen usually wore a haubergeon and cervelliere, but were sometimes further protected by plate on the shoulders, elbows and knees and shins, as were dismounted sergeants and burghers employed in the defence of castles or town walls.

From the above it may be seen that by 1340–1350 the knight was so weighed down with all the additional defences that rapid movement was exceedingly difficult. Therefore during this period some attempt was made to lighten the load by the use of *cuir bouilli* and horn in place of iron, especially on the lower part of the leg, these materials being shaped in the same style as the metal.

Plate Armour, 1350–1420

Having gained at last – and at some cost – an adequate protection against the weapons of the time, the mounted man was now faced with the English longbow, against which reinforced mail armour was useless at close range, for the deadly shafts could pierce gambeson, mail and aketon, and all too often found their way between or even through the plates of the coat of plates. Therefore, from 1350 on, in most parts of northern and western Europe, mail began to decline as the main form of defence and plate armour came to the fore. However, mail continued to be used, especially to guard the joints in plate armour; this being achieved by wearing an arming doublet which had gussets of mail attached at the armpits, inside of the elbows, and a stiff mail collar; and mail hose continued to be used by many knights. By the end of the 1350s therefore a complete, smooth-fitting armour of plate had been developed which was 75% effective at keeping out the English arrows, although naturally a great variety of armour continued to be worn during the century, since many knights were too poor to afford the expensive plate armour, while others saw little active service and were content with their old armour.

It is significant that sometime between 1350 and 1360 the cyclas was replaced by the skirted jupon, another sleeveless, hip-length garment of leather or padded textile with a scalloped bottom edge. (The surcoat and cyclas continued to be worn until c. 1370, presumably with the old styles of body armour.) The jupon was closer fitting than its predecessors, laced up at the sides and needed no belt to gather it in at the waist. It was worn until c. 1425, when it was discarded to reveal solid breast and back plates, evolved from the coat of plates during the period 1340–1370. Those knights who wore breastplates beneath their jupons may be identified by their distinctive 'waisted' shape.

The first step towards a breastplate was the merging of some of the smaller plates on the upper half of the chest into a solid plate. Such small breastplates are first mentioned in 1340 but the first illustrated examples do not appear until the 1360s. The small plates below this breastplate were also merged into larger plates so that by *c.* 1361 the jupon contained or covered three long plates arranged horizontally at the front, and another three at the rear, overlapping each other from the bottom up to provide some degree of flexibility, and meeting at the sides. Gradually the size of the top-plate on the breast was enlarged until it covered the entire breast and reached down to the waist, a fauld of overlapping lames riveted to a leather skirt protecting the wearer below the waist. This breastplate was globular in shape and, with the front skirt, was secured over a haubergeon by straps crossing at the back. Many German knights still had only quilted defences as late as 1386, with no sign of a breastplate.

Another new piece of equipment in the late 1360s was the lance rest, riveted to the right side of the breastplate, which gave the knight greater control over his lance. Lance rests were in common use by 1380. In the 1360s chains began to be used on weapons and helmet, fastened to mamelieres, small metal discs on the breastplate. There were usually three such chains, for sword, dagger and helmet, the last being carried slung over the shoulder, and this practice suggests that by this date squires had become so much an integral part of the cavalry that they could no longer be expected to be at hand to replenish lost or broken weapons.

By 1390 a vee-shaped ridge of metal had been fixed to the breastplate just below the curve of the neck to prevent the point of a weapon sliding up to the throat. This was called a stop rib and similar ribs soon appeared on the arm and leg plates. By 1400 the plates forming the defence for the back were merged into a single backplate so that the upper body was now encased in a solid shell of iron. Backplates were in general use from 1420.

At the turn of the century the spaudler developed into a large curved plate known as a pauldron. These were worn

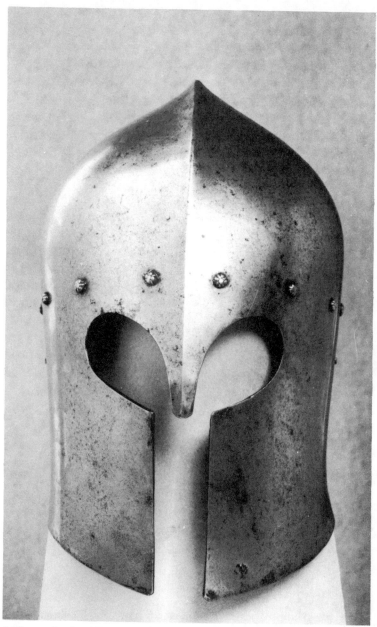

Milanese barbute in Corinthian style, about 1445.

Fourteenth century bascinet from northern Italy. The hooks and hole above the face opening were probably for a nasal bar.

in pairs at each shoulder, one at the front and one at the back, and overlapped the breast and back plates to form a really solid shoulder defence. The right pauldron was smaller than the left to allow for the lance. Shoulder defences of plate remained rare in Italy until about 1420. The couters were also enlarged, usually in a shell or heart shape, to protect the tendons more fully, and that for the bridle arm was especially elaborate. Mitten gauntlets with large plates across the fingers replaced the gauntlet with separate fingers. The rerebrace and vambrace remained simple but practical, consisting of two gutter-shaped plates hinged on the outside and buckled on the inside. The defences for the leg were basically the same as in 1370 and remained unchanged until about 1430.

The Shield, 1360–1500

The shield had been used less and less by mounted men since the 1360s but those which were used took on fancy shapes, such as the bouché shield, which had a ridge running down the middle to deflect blows and a notch in the top right hand corner to allow greater freedom of movement for the lance. The bouché came into general use at the end of the fourteenth century, as did several other designs which curved or were angled towards the enemy at top and bottom to prevent a lance being deflected into the head or groin, but the heater remained the most popular form of shield except in Spain and Portugal, where the shields were more rectangular with a curved bottom edge. During the early fifteenth century the shield gradually went out of use altogether amongst mounted men and after about 1450 was rarely used except for tournaments. Infantry still used pavises, targes and bucklers, though less frequently, most only carrying the larger types of shield when attacking fortifications.

The Helmet, 1350–1400

The conical bascinet had remained the most common type of helmet throughout the second half of the fourteenth century but during that time various forms of visor had been developed in an attempt to give full protection to the face, although in Italy and Germany many knights were content with a nasal bar attached to the brow of the helmet. By the 1350s the Germans had produced the Klappvisier, with long horizontal vision slits and breathing holes, which was hinged at the brow of the helmet. From this developed the snout-shaped visor with side fastenings; the characteristic helmet of the late fourteenth, early fifteenth centuries. At first rather blunt, the visor was later made more angular and pointed to deflect blows. The globular bascinet, popular in France and Italy, rarely had a visor. The kettle hat remained popular and was sometimes worn over the bascinet as an extra defence.

At the turn of the century the apex of the bascinet was moved back so that the rear of the helmet was almost perpendicular. About the same time the apex and the visor became more rounded and by 1410 the old pattern bevor and gorget of plate had been re-introduced to replace the aventail. Later the bevor became part of the helmet to form what is known as the great bascinet.

Fifteenth Century Plate Armour

When the bevor and gorget replaced the aventail the knight was finally encased in armour made entirely of plate – although mail continued to be used throughout this century – and the craft of the armourer was entering its finest period, reaching its peak in the second half of the century. Armour had originally been made by blacksmiths, but in the first part of the 14th century the call for more and more plate armour had caused the emergence of the craft of the armourer, with the various plate defences designed to respond to the movements of the body, riveted together in such a

Pavises carried by a horizontal handle shaped like a capital I. The true archer's pavise had a prop to enable it to be stood up when firing. That on the left bears *Argent*, a castle *Sable*, perhaps Ravensburg in Württemberg; the right-hand one bears the arms of Nuremberg. About 1490.

way as to give the maximum flexibility and with slots to allow plates to slide over each other.

An average equipment of plate armour of the early fifteenth century, known as 'all white' armour because it was

47

Bascinet, probably Italian, *c.* 1390–1400, with the visor pinned to pivots at the side.

highly burnished and not covered by the jupon, might weigh between 60 and 70 lb., but a trained man could carry out normal activities without strain in such a harness: experiments by the New York Metropolitan Museum have shown that a man in full plate armour can run, jump, lie down on his face or back and rise without undue trouble, and both Edward I and Henry V of England are recorded to have been able to leap into the saddle without using their stirrups. The British infantryman at the Somme in 1916 carried 60 lb. on his back, but the weight of a plate equipment was carefully distributed and balanced over the whole body by accurate fitting. The main disadvantage of plate armour was *not* its weight, but its stuffiness, for the lack of air and the sweat caused by the hot sun or physical exertion were far more exhausting than wearing and moving in the armour.

Plate armour was manufactured from bars of iron, hammered out with sledge hammers into thick plates, and the individual pieces then beaten to shape with a variety of hammers and small anvils. The pieces were frequently softened in a charcoal furnace during this process and the result was a wrought iron with a skin of steel which was often almost equal in quality to modern tool steel. The iron was kept thickest where the plate would face the enemy, i.e. the front of the head, the chest and on the left side. The edges were trimmed by huge shears and, where they formed the outer edge of a defence, stiffened by rolling them round a· wire to form a stop rib which made the edge less liable to damage and prevented thrusting weapons being deflected into a vital part. The pieces were then smoothed on grindstones and polished. Some were decorated at the edges with brass or silver, or with punched designs, and in the later fifteenth century it was usual to turn the steel a deep blue colour by re-tempering it after the polishing stage.

The pieces were then assembled with rivets, leaving a certain amount of play or providing sliding slots, lames being riveted to a leather strap on the inside. As far as possible all plates overlapped away from the expected point of attack. Finally the armour was proofed by firing a crossbow bolt at it at fairly close range.

The great iron-producing centres of Europe were northern Italy and southern Germany and it was in these two areas that the greatest armour industries developed; Milan

and Pisa in particular in Italy, Augsburg, Landshut, Nuremberg and Innsbruck in Germany. (Nuremberg specialised in
producing munition armour; armour for the ordinary
soldiers which was much less substantial.) Later many
Italians emigrated to Tours, Flanders and to England.

Because armour was produced mainly in two regions of
Europe, there developed two distinct styles, each influencing
the other, and therefore the styles often becoming combined
in one equipment. Both styles were exported, different
styles being produced when required to suit the taste of the
importing country, and armourers in other countries also
produced styles derived from the Italian and German ones.
Germany probably exported more armour than Italy, yet
the Italian armourers also made equipments in the Gothic
style and exported them to Germany. France seems to have
followed mainly the Italian fashions; Flanders, Spain and
Portugal a blending of the two styles, although in these last
three countries cuirasses of brigandine were frequently used
instead of plate.

Italian armourers had founded a thriving industry by the
fourteenth century, especially in Milan, and once a knight
was armed cap-à-pied, by between 1410–1420, they began
experimenting to perfect the full plate equipment. The first
step was to divide the breastplate once more to give greater
flexibility and this was done by shortening the plate slightly
and adding an overlapping plate, the placate – only a few
inches deep, which curved to a point at the top and fastened
to the breastplate with a strap. A similar plate was used at
the back. During the century the placate became larger and
more pointed until it covered almost the whole breast. The
backplate also increased slightly in size and from c. 1450 was
divided into three or four horizontally overlapping lames
to give even greater flexibility. The fauld of lames was
altered c. 1430 so that the lower lame was separated into two
parts at the front by a semi-circular gap, and divided at the
sides from the rear lame. All three of these plates, called
tassets, were attached to the lame above by straps. By about

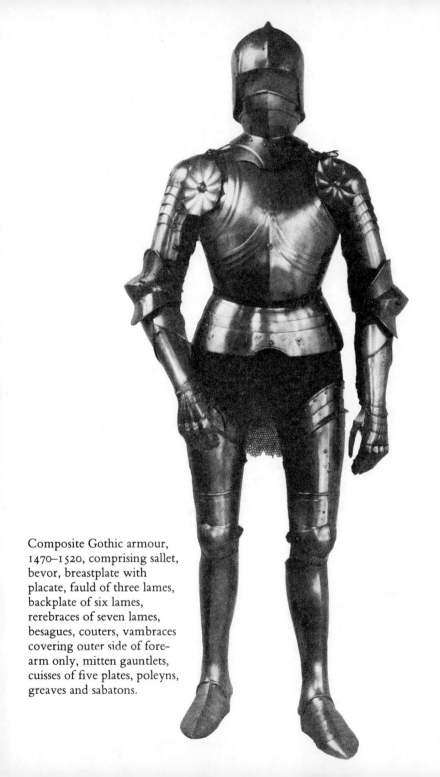

Composite Gothic armour,
1470–1520, comprising sallet,
bevor, breastplate with
placate, fauld of three lames,
backplate of six lames,
rerebraces of seven lames,
besagues, couters, vambraces
covering outer side of forearm only, mitten gauntlets,
cuisses of five plates, poleyns,
greaves and sabatons.

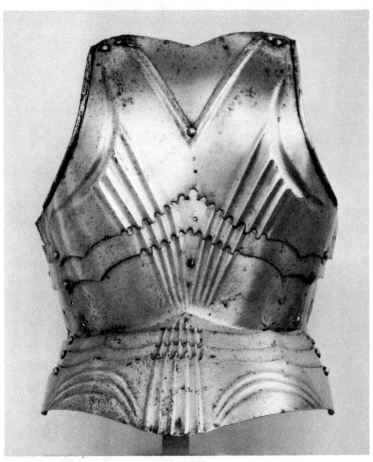

Gothic backplate of seven plates, *c.* 1470.

1450 the fore tassets were extended down the thighs, taking on a triangular shape, and the breast and back plates and the fauld were joined to make one piece of armour or a cuirass, hinged on the left and buckled together on the right. Italian armours frequently had a mail skirt instead of the fauld described above, and mail sabatons were also common.

Milanese globular breastplate of about 1500–1520. The two large holes are for the bolts of a lance rest.

Pauldrons were large and round, and from c. 1430 had their inner edges turned up to protect the neck from a side cut. These turn-ups were called haute-pieces. A large circular plate was sometimes added as a reinforcement in front of the left pauldron and by about mid-century this had developed into garde braces which fitted partly over both pauldrons and bore the haute-pieces. The large back pauldrons were at first almost rectangular but by the 1470s had become pointed and overlapped each other at the back. By 1500 the haute-pieces had been increased in size, the left one standing nearly as high as the ear.

Italian armour was characterised by its smooth, rounded lines. German armour, with a distinctive slim and rather spiky yet graceful form, began to be produced about 1460 and remained popular until the end of the century, reaching a quality equal to the best Italian armour by about 1475. The breastplate was in two parts and the backplate laminated, but sometimes two or more placates were used. However, by the end of the century the breastplate was once more a single plate, with a globular shape. The fauld was short and often of mail. Sabatons were always of plate and had very long toes. Towards the end of the century the toes became so long, in imitation of civilian fashion, that it was difficult to walk in the sabatons and the long toes were fixed on by means of locking pins after the knight had mounted. Shoulder defences were large, following the advances made

German gauntlet of about 1480 with typical pointed cuff and Gothic fluting.

by the Italians, and gauntlets had long pointed cuffs, the fingers now protected by a single broad plate. The edges of the various plates were cut in graceful curves and often edged with brass pierced with tracery. Fluting was used to decorate and strengthen the whole equipment, this fluting becoming more and more extravagant as the end of the century drew near.

Fifteenth Century Helmets

The great bascinet remained common in Germany during the fifteenth century, the aventail replaced by plates which were strapped to the body armour so that the helmet did not move with the head, but in general the bascinet was replaced in the early fifteenth century by a helmet known as the armet, a closed helmet consisting of the simple rounded cap of the bascinet with two cheek pieces which overlapped at the front when closed and were hinged at the top edge. By mid-century most had detachable visors, a reinforcing plate above the brow, and a plate called a wrapper to protect the face more. This last plate was fitted around the cheek pieces and also covered part of the chest, being secured to the helmet at the back by a strap. By about 1460 the skull was ridged to strengthen it and as the century went on the face opening became larger. The great bascinet continued to be worn, but only for tournaments. The armet first appeared about 1416 in Germany, although it is believed to have been of Italian origin. It was in general use by the 1420s and remained popular throughout Europe that century, though the style varied slightly from country to country. It was less popular in England than elsewhere.

The kettle hat fell from favour in Italy but remained very popular in Germany, often now having a small crown and an acutely turned down brim in which a gap was cut to allow vision. The bevor was still worn with the kettle hat to protect the face and this combination became more popular until it was universally adopted towards the end of the century.

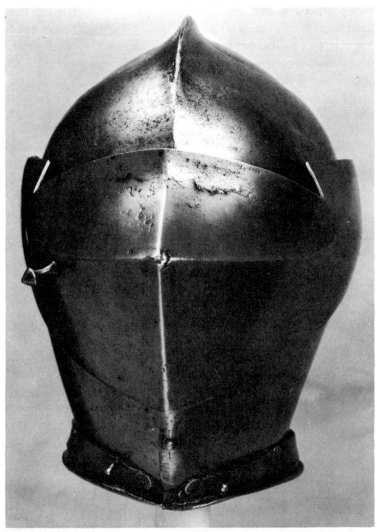

Italian armet, late fifteenth – early sixteenth century.

In mid-century the bascinet also gave rise to a style of helmet called ˌthe sallet, which originated in Italy. The Italian sallet had a slightly bell shape˙with a pointed neck guard and long horizontal vision slits in a fixed visor. It was worn in conjunction with the bevor, which was usually secured to the breastplate. The German sallet was generally more rounded over the brow and had a long, laminated tail. The front was sometimes formed by a separate visor. The more rounded German type was most common in northern and western Europe; in England, where the sallet was very popular, a style midway between the two was adopted.

After about 1480 the German sallet had a very short tail and a close fitting skull, with a flat, pivoted visor. Another style which developed about the same time was the open faced sallet, which ran in a steep slope from the brow to an extended tail. The Spanish cabacete also became popular in these last two decades. This was a tall, narrow helmet with a turned down brim which was drawn up to a point at front and rear. It was worn with a large bevor that came up to the nose, the gorget part extending down on to the chest.

War-hat from Augsburg, similar to the Spanish cabacete.

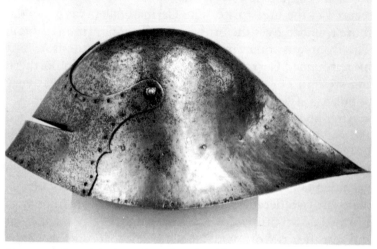

German sallet with visor pivoted at the sides, *c*. 1480–1510.

Fifteenth Century Equipments

The full plate equipment was very expensive and not all that easy to obtain. The great princes and nobles had such equipments, and princes often gave full equipments of plate as gifts, but for the simple knight and the rank and file of the armies there was little chance of obtaining a full plate equipment, unless it were taken on the battlefield. Therefore, in the second half of the fifteenth century, mail, or mail with partial plate, continued to be used extensively. Foot soldiers in particular relied on the old combination of fabric and metal, topped by a bascinet, kettle hat or sallet, the latter being very popular but usually of a shallower pattern than that worn by knights. The jack was the most common form of body armour, being cheaper than the brigandine, and was sometimes reinforced by the addition of plate – always to the upper half of the body, for the legs were not threatened by mounted men and agility was as important as defensive armour. Archers usually wore a short sleeved haubergeon or brigandine, but are often portrayed wearing

German sallet forged from one piece, about 1450–1460.

a breastplate, or sometimes just a deep placate; no doubt the
spoils of war. There was no leg armour for these men and
they wore an open helmet until the arrival of the sallet.
Crossbowmen wore similar defences but often had the full
breastplate and placate, and occasionally even a fauld of
plate. Vambraces and poleyns were worn on rare occasions.
The Swiss pikemen, again mostly because of poverty, wore
simple steel caps and breastplates, many having only leather
jerkins. Backplates, leg and arm pieces were so rare that
there were usually only enough fully armoured men to
form a single rank at the head of the phalanx. Towards the
end of the century sallets were worn and a larger percentage
of men had half armour. Hose and tunics were striped or
particoloured but were tight fitting, without the slashing so
common in the following century. In the main the Landsknechts were also unarmoured, wearing leather or fabric
armour and simple steel caps or mail caps under hats. Other
clothing resembled that of the Swiss. The Spanish infantryman of the second half of the century wore full armour on
body, legs and arms, with a cabacete and bevor on his head,

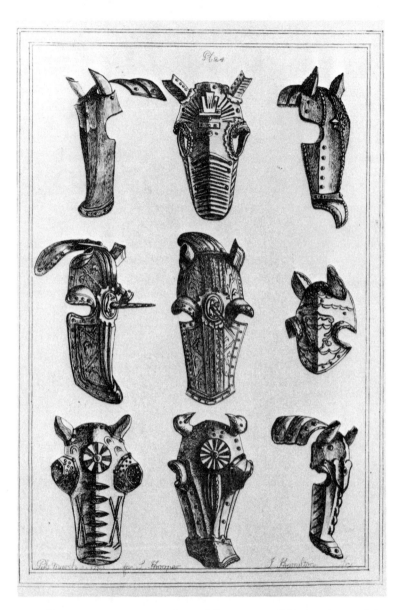

Chanfrons. The first two in the middle row are different views of the same chanfron, both bearing a ragged staff device and therefore perhaps belonging to the Earl of Warwick.

Horse armour worn until *c.* 1400: iron chanfron, mail crinet, a peytral of what appears to be scale armour, and leather over the flanks and hind quarters.

Two views of Gothic war harness for man and horse, made at Landshut about 1475–1485. Note the coarse felt and canvas linings.

and carried a buckler: it was this full armour which made him so deadly at close quarters with the Swiss.

Horse Armour

Examples of horse caparisons of fabric may be seen as early as the end of the twelfth century. These coverings

were divided into two parts which met at the saddle. They
were apparently of cloth, being full and loose, and reached
down to the horse's fetlocks. Most covered the horse's head
as well as its body, although some ended behind the horse's
ears. The purpose of these coverings is now uncertain but it

is believed that they were designed to prevent light infantry from hamstringing the horses with their long knives and the spearmen from galling the horses with their spears. By the first quarter of the thirteenth century the fabric was being reinforced with plates of horn or metal. Leather and quilted caparisons were also in use, and about the same date there is the first reference to horse armour of iron, probably the chanfron, or head-plate, which was now coming into general use. The chanfron might cover the entire head, or be just a plate on the face. Some had spikes protruding from the forehead.

Mail caparisons appeared in mid-thirteenth century and these were in two parts like their predecessors, but with the front part shortened to knee level because of the excessive weight. However, mail caparisons were rare because of weight and cost, and leather or quilting remained the most common material. By about 1300 there is mention of the peytral, or breastplate, of iron or *cuir bouilli*.

Mail caparisons appear rarely during the fourteenth century and those seen are usually shortened all round. Leather and quilted caparisons remained in common use, sometimes reinforced by a chanfron and a laminated neck-piece of plate known as a crinet, which was originally only a crest for the horse but developed to cover the whole neck. Some of the textile caparisons now finished just above the horse's shoulders, leaving neck and head to be protected by the plate armour.

The textile caparison gradually went out of use towards the end of the century and the pieces of plate armour took over, although these pieces were often of *cuir bouilli* instead of iron in the interests of lightness. During the first half of the fifteenth century the horse's furnishings were in-fluenced by the increasing use of plate and after about 1450 in addition to the chanfron, crinet and peytral, plates began to be fitted to the saddle to protect the flanks of the horse (flanchards) and along the horse's back (the crupper). The latter sometimes had a spike on it to prevent light infantry jumping up behind the knight. The ensemble of pieces of plate was known as a bard. Because of the cost and weight of plate armour, leather pieces remained popular for horse armour throughout the fifteenth century.

Saddlery

The saddle of the knight was designed to enable the rider almost to stand in it so that the greatest impact might be delivered with the lance. This meant that the cantle and pommel of the saddle, the arsons or arçons, were very high and were curved round the rider's hips to give extra support and protection. The breast band was sometimes strapped round the rear arçon, and double girths were used to support the saddle against the impact, one girth sometimes passing over the top of the saddle. In the second half of the fifteenth century the arçons were reinforced by iron plates.

Stirrup leathers were long to allow the rider to brace his legs forward at full length with straight knees, his feet well home in the stirrups and his body braced against the cantle. Italian stirrups were often of iron, in a bucket shape, to provide extra protection for the feet, Italian armours normally having mail sabatons.

Left to right: *estoc*, or arming sword, of *c.* 1400 with fig-shaped pommel and diamond section blade; French sword of *c.* 1340 with wheel pommel and blade with fuller; French estoc of 1375–1400 with wheel pommel and diamond section blade with ricasso; French estoc about 1350–1400 with wheel pommel and flattened diamond section blade.

CHAPTER THREE

Weapons

The Sword

AT the beginning of the fourteenth century weapons were
divided into two distinct classes; the knightly weapons of
lance and sword, with occasionally the axe or mace, and the
weapons of the lower classes such as the spear, axe, bow and
crossbow. The sword in particular was regarded as the
special weapon of the nobility. At this period the armoured
horseman dominated the battlefield and the main role of the
infantry was to support cavalry charges. No infantryman
could afford a knight's sword, nor would the lords have
allowed him to carry one, the sword being the symbol or
badge of rank of a knight at that time. Instead infantrymen
carried a long knife, although sometimes archers had a
crude short sword called a falchion. Should an infantryman
obtain a knight's sword on the field of battle he was unlikely to encumber himself with such a large weapon, the
sword after all being a secondary weapon for infantry. This
situation was to change during the fourteenth century as the
sword, and indeed all weapons, began to be developed in
various specialised styles to combat the increasing use of
plate armour defences.

At the end of the thirteenth century there was only one type of sword, apart from the falchion mentioned above, and this remained similar to that of Viking times; a blade between 33 and 36 inches long, flat and wide, and tapering slightly from the hilt to form an obtuse point. A broad central groove – the fuller – ran almost the full length of the blade, serving to lighten it yet maintain rigidity. The hilt was formed by long quillons of iron which curved slightly towards the blade; a wooden grip covered with leather, parchment or cloth and bound with wire, cord or leather thong, to provide a good hold; and the pommel to counterbalance the weight of the blade. A small button of metal was placed on top of the pommel to protect it when the end of the tang was hammered over, though sometimes the tang was threaded to receive a nut. The type of pommel predominant at the beginning of the fourteenth century was that known as the wheel pommel, originally just a flat disc of metal, but by now having a hub-like protuberance on each side of the disc, the face of which was frequently decorated with the family seal. The wheel pommel remained popular throughout the fourteenth and fifteenth centuries. Swords of this type weighed 3–4 lb. and when swung with a stiff arm action were capable of literally shearing off a head or limb.

The first major changes are noticeable by 1320, by which date most knights were wearing plate defences on arms and legs. At this date the sword was longer, under the theory that the longer the blade the heavier the blow and the greater the chance of smashing the new defences. The new swords had four-foot blades, tapering gradually to a point, with seven-inch grips which enabled both hands to be used to put even greater force behind a blow, although the swords were not too large to be wielded with one hand. These swords are known as hand-and-a-half swords, though contemporary records refer to them simply as swords of war, or long swords. They remained popular throughout the fourteenth century, being especially suitable for fighting

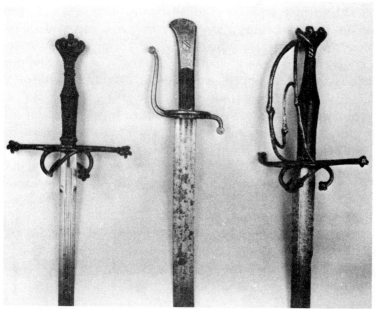

Left and right: German long (hand-and-a-half) swords of the early sixteenth century, similar to those in use in the late fifteenth century; centre, sixteenth century German sabre with falchion type blade and hilt of style used for infantry swords in the second half of the fifteenth century.

on foot, which was a predominant tactic with the French after Crécy in 1346. The pommel was usually of a conical or triangular shape, larger than the wheel pommel, the extra weight being necessary to counter-balance the longer blade. The conical shape remained common until mid-fifteenth century. The average weight of these swords was $4\frac{1}{2}$–5 lb.

The second development was a marked rise in the popularity of the falchion. As we have seen, this had been used mostly by archers, presumably because it was a convenient length and weight, and it continued to be used throughout the fourteenth and fifteenth centuries by infantry and some mounted men, but from c. 1320–1340 it became very popular amongst mounted men, probably because of its great cleaving power.

The falchion had a curved, sharpened edge and a heavy, straight and blunt back edge, the two meeting in a sharp point. Many were very broad towards the point in order to concentrate more force behind a blow. Occasionally the back edge was 'clipped' at the point to give the sword a slightly hooked appearance, and towards the end of the century this curving of the blade became more pronounced. A few examples occur of falchions fitted to short hafts, 18–24 in. long, no doubt to increase reach and swing. The hilts were similar to those of the other swords, though in the second half of the century the triangular pommel became

Sixteenth century falchion of Cosimo de' Medici. Plainer swords of this style were used by infantry after about 1450.

more kite shaped, this remaining a popular style until early in the next century.

By the second half of the fourteenth century plate armour was being used so extensively, and protected the wearer so efficiently, that an entirely new type of sword began to appear; the thrusting sword, or *estoc*. In cross-section the blades of these new swords were either an elongated diamond or a flattened hexagonal shape, in both cases without a fuller. These narrow, stiff blades, tapering to a very sharp point, were designed solely for thrusting at the chinks in armour. Contemporary illustrations often show the estoc being held against the shoulder, rather like a lance or spear, and in the fifteenth century these swords were frequently without sharpened edges, making them entirely a thrusting weapon.

Such swords, aiming for small cracks in an opponent's

armour, needed much finer control than the earlier slashing swords, and to achieve this knights began to hook their forefingers over the base of the blade, above the crossguard. About 1360 that part of the blade, the ricasso, was left blunt for between one and two inches. This gave rise, at the end of the century, to a bar branching out from the front half of the guard and curving round in a loop to protect the forefinger. The estoc remained popular in the next century but never replaced the slashing sword, which continued to be used alongside it.

At about the same date, the 1360s, the sword was frequently attached to the breastplate by a light chain about $3\frac{1}{2}$ ft. long, secured to the grip by a ring. This practice does not seem to have lasted long, and a more common method was the sword knot, a loop of leather thong or silk cord secured to the grip and slipped over the wrist.

Amongst the infantry swords were still comparatively rare at this date – at Poitiers in 1356 the English archers fought hand-to-hand with their mauls or weapons picked up from the ground. Spearmen usually relied on long knives as a secondary weapon and could create havoc with horses at close quarters. However, more swords were now being carried at the belt by infantry, especially the archers and crossbowmen, and these seem to have been mainly the early slashing swords.

Towards the end of the century knights began to carry two swords; the long sword, hung from the saddle, and the shorter estoc, often called the arming sword now, which was carried at the belt. By 1420 every knight was armed with these two swords. The blade of the long sword was still broad and rather flat, with a strengthening rib up the centre of each side. However, by the mid-fifteenth century full plate armour had become so expensive that only the nobles and princes could afford it and many of the lesser knights reverted to mail with partial plate. This led to a return of the old-style slashing sword, but keeping a sharp point.

These types of blade remained unchanged for the rest of the fifteenth century, but there were changes in the hilt. The conical pommel became pear-shaped in mid-century and about the same date the wheel pommel reverted to a plain flat disc. These were now the two most common forms of pommel. Also in mid-century a second branch developed from the crossguard, forming a ring above the rear half of the guard, this and the first loop being known as the arms of the hilt.

By *c.* 1450 almost all infantry were armed with swords, though still as a secondary weapon. The Swiss pikemen carried a short sword for close quarters fighting, as did crossbowmen and archers. The later Landsknechts also carried a short, straight slashing sword with a rather obtuse point. Many of these infantry swords were single-edged weapons of the falchion type and during the 1450s the front half of the crossguard was turned towards the pommel to form a knuckle bow and the rear half towards the blade. Towards the end of the century the Spanish infantry came into prominence, armed with buckler and a short, straight, double-edged thrusting sword.

The shield had now been abandoned by mounted men and towards the end of the century many knights began to abandon their gauntlets. This led to the sword hilt developing a more complicated guard to defend the hand, and by the last quarter of the century the hilt usually consisted of the crossguard, the arms of the hilt, a knuckle bow and rings – or occasionally solid plates – on either side of the crossguard.

Towards the end of the fourteenth century the long sword had developed into the two handed sword with a 50 in. blade and 12 in. grip. This had not been very popular, mainly because of the space needed to wield it effectively. The sword could be shortened by grasping it with one hand above the hilt, this part of the blade being left blunt. In the late fifteenth century these swords returned to favour, mainly with the Swiss and Landsknechts, the bearers being known as double pay men (doppelsöldner), responsible for guarding the cantonal or company flag. The blunt part of the blade was now covered by a leather sheath and hooked lugs stuck out to serve as secondary quillons. The two-handed sword also occurred occasionally in Italy, where it had a sharp thrusting point.

Scabbards

Sword scabbards were made of two thin pieces of wood, shaped to fit the outline of the blade, then covered with parchment, leather or textile, which was glued to the wood and sewn either down the middle of the inner face or along one edge. To protect the point of the scabbard and sword a metal fitting known as a chape·was riveted to the bottom end of the scabbard.

In the first quarter of the fourteenth century the main method of wearing the sword and scabbard was on a belt looped loosely round the waist so that the sword hung on the left hip, the chape canted slightly to the rear. Until 1310 the belt was fastened to the scabbard with leather laces, but after·that date two metal bands were fitted at the top of the scabbard, one a few inches lower than the other, and to these bands were attached rings. These fittings were known as lockets and they enabled the scabbard to be attached to the belt by cords or chains with spring clips.

A second method used by some knights was a wide belt, worn low on the hips and often made of brooch-like links, sometimes decorated with jewels. This style became the predominant one for knights in the middle of the century and remained so for the next hundred years. The sword was still worn on the left hip, straight up and down, usually balanced by a dagger on the right hip. The scabbards of both were probably attached to the belt by small hooks.

In the first quarter of the fifteenth century the wide belt tended to be worn at more of an angle, and for battle many knights used just a metal ring on the belt to slide their estoc through, thus avoiding entangling their legs with the scabbard when fighting on foot. From *c.*1450 the early narrow belt worn loosely round the waist reappeared, but with the sword tilted more acutely to the rear. By the end of the century this style had been simplified to two straps of different lengths suspended from a waist belt with a third, diagonal strap to prevent the sword swinging about.

In the second half of the century another method began to be used by knights, probably originating in Germany in the 1450s. Plate armour now covered the hips and the scabbard was often fastened directly to the armour, making the belt obsolete. The scabbard was attached on the left side, straight up and down, and at the same height as if the hip belt were being worn. This style was widespread by 1480.

The Lance

Early cavalry spears were similar to infantry ones but by 1300 a distinct type of spear for cavalrymen had begun to evolve. This consisted of an ash or cypress shaft from 12–14 ft. long, topped by a small, slender head of steel. Early in the century there was added to the shaft, just behind where it was gripped by the hand, a metal ring called the graper. This ring was pressed against the shoulder and armpit when charging in order to prevent the lance being forced back under the arm with the shock of impact. During the 1380s, by which time the graper was in general use, a metal bracket called an arrest was bolted to the right side of the breast-plate to take some of the weight of the lance, and the graper rested against this. The term arrest became corrupted to rest, and lance 'rests' were common from 1400 onwards.

Some fourteenth century illustrations and monuments show a short crossguard in front of the hand. Towards the end of the century this was replaced by a small metal plate known as the avant plate or vamplate. However, the vamplate did not come into general use until *c.* 1425, by which date it was also much larger. About this date the butt end of the shaft

Left: poleaxe of about 1470. Right: poleaxe *c.* 1400–1450.

was thickened and the shaft tapered gradually to the point, and because of this the handgrip between vamplate and graper had to be made thinner to fit the hand comfortably, creating a distinct handgrip. Sergeants, squires and hobilars retained the simple, lighter spear. The Spanish light cavalry must have had a shorter version more like a javelin, for they frequently threw their 'lances' at the enemy.

The Poleaxe

At Agincourt, and on many other occasions, the knights broke off approximately six feet of their lances to use them as spears when fighting on foot, and from the mid-fifteenth century this, and the increasing effectiveness of infantry pole-arms, caused the evolution of a weapon for use by dismounted men-at-arms, known as the poleaxe.

The poleaxe consisted of a small axe head mounted on a 4–5 ft. haft with a spike at each end and a hammer head at the rear of the axe blade. Narrow steel strips, known as langets, were nailed to each side of the top of the haft to prevent the head of the weapon being chopped off, and a steel disc was fitted about 18 in. below the head to protect the upper hand. One version known as the Lucerne hammer, popular amongst the Swiss, had the axe part omitted and the hammer head was given three curved prongs instead. These weapons were wielded with both hands, the haft used for parrying, and could land a heavy blow capable of breaking open the strongest armour. They continued to be used by dismounted men-at-arms until the discarding of plate armour made them obsolete.

Maces and War Hammers

The primitive mace or club was used as an infantry weapon by the peasant levies throughout the fourteenth century and in the first half of the fifteenth century a form known as the 'Morning Star' was still employed by Swiss armies.

This mace, or club, was about 5 ft long with a head studded with iron spikes. It disappeared by mid-century. A weapon of the same name, but consisting of a spiked ball attached to a haft by a chain, was used by the Flemish infantry in the fifteenth century. English archers often carried a mallet or maul, a combination of tool and weapon which sometimes had a spike added to the top. The haft was about 4 ft long and the head was often of lead, making it a very effective weapon even against fully armoured men. The maul was really a general purpose agricultural tool used, amongst

Left to right: Milanese mace of Morning Star type; war hammer c. 1450; Gothic style mace of about 1470; Italian war hammer c. 1490; sixteenth century Italian mace.

other things, for stake-driving and breaking up clods of earth.

Mounted men used smaller versions of the mace, adopted from eastern Europe, as secondary weapons and during the fourteenth century the most usual form was an iron head with seven flanges projecting from it radially and a spike at the top, mounted on a wooden haft about 2 ft long. The flanges were somewhat triangular in shape. These maces were slung from the saddle by a leather thong and weighed from 4–6 pounds. By the early fifteenth century maces were made entirely of metal, with a disc on the haft to protect the hand.

The mace went out of fashion in the 1460s when it became lighter and more elegant, weighing between 2–3 lb., with acutely pointed flanges. It was found these flanges became stuck in any armour they penetrated and about 1490 the older form of mace reappeared and the weapon became popular again.

War hammers, consisting of a 24–30 in. metal haft with a

Fourteenth century axe-head, early fifteenth century mace-head.

3 in. hammer head backed by a spike, appeared in the last quarter of the fourteenth century and remained popular as a secondary or extra weapon for cavalry throughout the fifteenth century, again suspended from the saddle. Some of the hammers from eastern Europe had a long narrow spike and these must have been extremely effective at piercing armour.

Axes

The two-handed axe of the Saxons and Vikings was popular as a weapon for dismounted men-at-arms throughout Europe until the end of the fifteenth century. Despite its size the head usually weighed only about 3 lb., and was on a 4 ft. haft. Langets strengthened the haft and there was often a spike at the top.

The horseman's axe was a smaller and lighter version, often with a pick or hammer head on the rear of the blade.

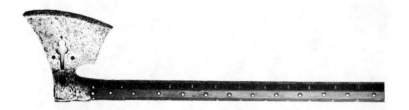

Late fifteenth century war-axe.

It became popular about the middle of the fifteenth century. In the late fourteenth century a throwing axe was also developed for use by cavalry which took the form of a cross, having four blades with a short handle and three spikes between them. This was thrown just before two sides met. (During the Hundred Years War maces, hammers, axes and daggers were often used as missiles when lines of dismounted men-at-arms approached each other).

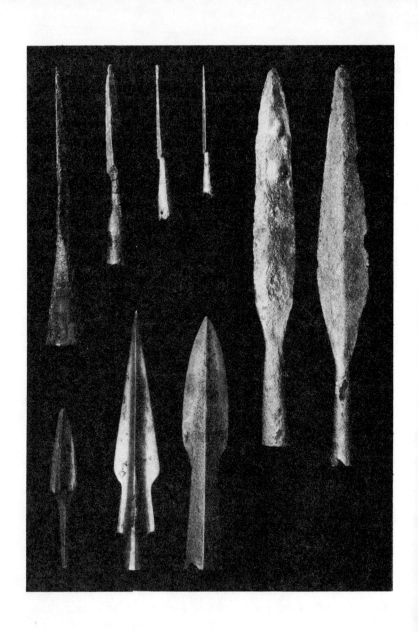

Selection of medieval spearheads found in London.

Staff Weapons

The spear was a major infantry weapon during the four-teenth century, used rather like a bayonet during a charge, or to form a hedge of points. The shaft was about 5 ft. long, topped by a 12 in. head, 2–3 in. wide at the base, with a strong rib running up the middle of the blade on each side. The weapon employed in close formation by the Scots and the Brabanters in the first half of the century was a longer version, with a smaller head, between 10–12 ft. long over-all. This was in effect an early pike.

By about 1300 it had become obvious that to overcome heavily armoured knights a more effective infantry staff weapon was required; a long-handled weapon which could be used for stabbing, or for a heavy cleaving blow capable of breaking through plate armour. This brought about a combination of the infantry spear and the axe to develop a whole range of infantry staff weapons. The thrusting point of the spear was nearly always retained, combined with the cutting edge of the axe or the peasant's bill hook, and the differences between the weapons were therefore mainly the predominance given to the cutting edge, as in the bill and halberd, and the point, as in the partizan and pike.

Bills

Agricultural bill-hooks on long hafts were used in the fourteenth century, but from the beginning of the fifteenth century it is noticeable that organised bodies of infantry formerly referred to as spearmen are now termed bill men. In this later bill the long, slightly hooked, cutting edge of the heavy agricultural bill-hook remained predominant, but a spike was added at the top, above the rear edge, from which a hook often projected. The haft was about 6 ft. long. This weapon remained popular throughout the fifteenth century, especially in England, France and Italy.

The glaive was a close relation of the bill, having a broad, single-edged blade, rather like a large knife blade, mounted on a 5 ft. haft, with a small hook occasionally added to the back of the blade. This weapon was also popular throughout the fifteenth century, especially in France, Germany and Spain.

The French infantry had another version of the bill, called a war scythe, which closely resembled the agricultural scythe but had a spike added to the back of the blade.

Halberds

The halberd first appeared in Switzerland during the thirteenth century under the name of voulge, which was nothing more than a heavy, 12 in.-long rectangular cleaving blade on a 7-ft. pole, with a long, thick spike at the top; the axe being the predominant feature in halberds. During the fourteenth century a stubby spike was added to the rear of the blade and in the fifteenth century the haft was reinforced by langets, but otherwise the halberd remained unchanged throughout the 1300–1500 period. The weapon was capable of delivering a blow of great force and even the heaviest armour was not always proof against it.

The gisarme was another form of halberd which remained popular until the late fifteenth century. This had a crescent-shaped blade secured to the haft at the centre, and sometimes also at the lower end where the tip of the blade curled round the haft to form a second socket. The bardiche or berdische of eastern Europe was of a similar design but the axe blade had less depth.

Partizans

The partizan was a development of the spear and originated in Italy early in the fifteenth century. It soon spread throughout Europe, being a particularly simple yet effective weapon with a 30-in. blade, very broad at the base and tapering to a point. Both edges were sharpened so that the

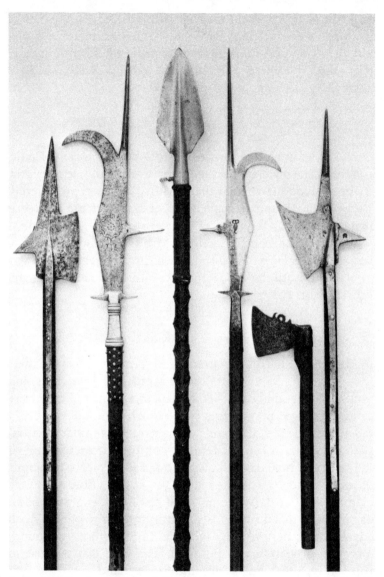

Left to right: Swiss halberd, late fourteenth century – early fifteenth century; sixteenth century Italian bills similar to style used in previous century, separated by a German boar spear *c.* 1600; fifteenth century war-axe; German halberd *c.* 1500, typical of the type carried by German and Swiss infantry in the late fifteenth century.

partizan could be used for either cut or thrust. At the base of the blade were two lugs, originally straight but later curving out and down, or pointing upwards as in the form known as the ranseur, where fork-like projections were used to entangle and break sword blades.

The Pike

Massed spearmen had formed an anti-cavalry force since the twelfth century but in the early fourteenth century the Swiss revived the ancient pike. At first this was no different to the Scottish and Brabançon spear but later the shaft was lengthened to 15 ft and to 18 ft by the late fifteenth century, with langets at least 24 in. long to prevent the head being cut off. A phalanx of such pikes was impregnable to cavalry attack and, until the end of the fifteenth century, against any other infantry.

Daggers and Knives

In the first half of the fourteenth century most daggers followed the shape of the sword and had long hilts and quillons and round or crescent-shaped pommels. These were called simply quillon daggers. Gradually they developed a tapered blade of diamond, sometimes triangular section, with a smaller crossguard and a pommel to match that of the sword. These daggers were designed to pierce the joints of an opponent's armour or the slits in his visor, and were primarily carried by knights. A distinct form of quillon dagger was that known as the Burgundian dagger, which had heraldic designs engraved on it and a hollow round, diamond or star-shaped pommel. The type was popular in Burgundy, northern France and Switzerland.

From about 1325 three distinct forms of military dagger and knife began to develop: the ballock knife, the ear dagger and the rondel dagger. The ballock knife appeared during the first quarter of the century and became especially

Left to right French
rondel dagger,
1440–1450; French
quillon dagger,
c. 1500; German
rondel dagger, early
sixteenth century;
Flemish kidney
dagger, about 1450–
1460; Venetian ear
dagger; German
rondel dagger,
about 1450.

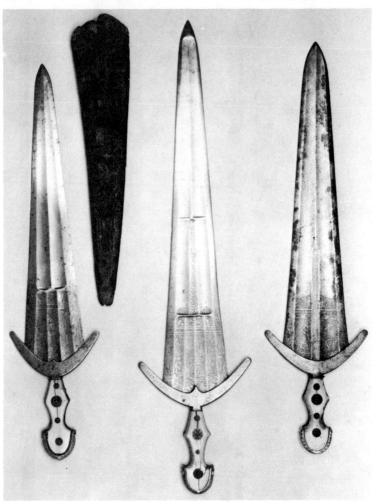

Cinquedea daggers or short swords from Ferrara; left to right: 1500, 1490, 1470.

popular in England and the Low Countries. It took its name from the hilt, which had two small lobes at the base of the blade to form the guard. The blade was usually narrow and pointed, normally single-edged but sometimes with a double edge.

The ear dagger was common throughout the 1300–1500 period and appears to have originated from the Near East, becoming very popular in Spain before spreading to France and England. This dagger also took its name from the hilt, which had two semi-circular discs projecting from the pommel at an angle. At first the ears were almost parallel to each other but late in the fifteenth century they opened out to a wider angle. Blade and hilt were often made from one piece of steel.

The rondel dagger also appeared in the first half of the fourteenth century. It had a blade of triangular section and a hilt with a rondel or disc shaped guard and a similar disc in place of a pommel. The blade might be long and slender – up to 20 in. in length – or short and thick, capable of punching through most armour. The shorter type was most popular from 1360 to 1410. The rondel dagger was used particularly by knights.

In the second half of the fifteenth century a dagger known as the cinquedea was introduced in Italy. It had a broad blade, said to be the width of five fingers, hence the name. The blade was from 18–22 in. long, tapering to a point, and was often fluted and finely etched. The hilt was frequently of ivory.

These daggers and knives were used by both infantry and cavalry. The shorter ones were used purely as daggers, with the point down, but the cinquedea and rondel in particular appear to have been used as short swords by infantry and by knights in a similar role when their sword had been lost or broken. The Welsh and Irish spearmen of the fourteenth century were especially noted for their long knives, which often wreaked havoc amongst the horses of the cavalry in a mêlée.

The Crossbow

The crossbow consisted of a short bow stave passed through a slot at one end of a straight stock (the tiller) and held in place by wedges and/or lashing. The thick bow 'string' of cord was held in the loaded or spanned position by a groove in a horizontally rotating catch (the nut) which was set into the tiller. The nut was prevented from rotating by a long Z-shaped trigger, the top and shorter end of which engaged in a notch in the underside of the nut. To release the nut the longer bottom bar of the trigger was pressed up to the tiller, disengaging the top bar from the notch and allowing the cord to turn the nut and release itself.

During the first half of the fourteenth century the most common form of crossbow was that fitted with a composite stave fashioned from layers of wood and horn. To span this bow the crossbowman had a hook attached to his belt, which he looped over the cord. He placed his foot in a metal stirrup set into the front end of the tiller and, placing his hands on the butt of the tiller, used the weight of his body to pull the cord back and engage the nut.

As early as 1315 the French replaced the composite bowstave with a more powerful one of steel, this type of crossbow being known as an arbalest, but the composite stave remained the most common type throughout the fourteenth century and much of the fifteenth. Arbalests became more common from the beginning of the fifteenth century but were not really popular until late in the century, the main reason being that they could not be spanned without mechanical aid, which greatly slowed down the loading process. There were two main types of spanning devices, the windlass and the cranequin. The windlass consisted of a metal framework, slipped over the butt of the tiller, which contained a spindle and two long cranked handles. Two cords with hooks at their ends were attached to the spindle and these were slipped over the bow cord and the handles turned to wind the cord back to the nut. The windlass could be hooked on the belt, but is often shown dropped to the ground at the crossbowman's feet. It was common from the early fifteenth century. The cranequin was a more substantial affair and consisted of a box of metal, permanently

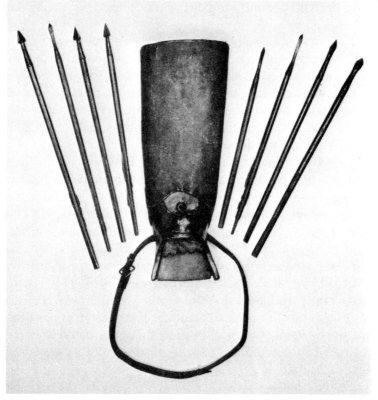

Crossbow quiver of wood covered with rawhide (lid missing), with bolts fledged with slivers of wood. German, about 1470.

fixed to the butt of the tiller, in which was a large cog turned by a long handle. The teeth of the cog engaged the teeth on the side of a bar running down the top of the tiller, at the end of which was a double hook to engage the bow cord. Once the cord had been pulled back over the nut by this device, the bar was wound down again to clear the cord and then removed.

Obviously the arbalest had a better range and penetration than the crossbow, but the delay caused by spanning greatly outweighed these advantages in the field and arbalests seem to have been used mainly in siege work. The arbalest weighed about 9 pounds.

The wooden bolts, or quarrels, for the crossbow were thick and short, oval in section, with two thin wooden, leather or parchment vanes to impart spin to the missile for greater accuracy. The bolts were tipped with short, solid iron heads of square or diamond section. A box quiver, secured to the waist belt, was used to house the bolts, usually having a narrow neck just below the vanes.

Maximum range for the composite bow was somewhere between 300 and 350 yd, for the arbalest about 380 to 400 yd, but neither was accurate much beyond 60 yd and effective range would probably have been more like 200 yd. The rate of fire was so slow that up to twelve longbow shafts could be released in the time it took to span and fire an arbalest, between four and six when loading a composite bow.

Crossbows were used to prove plate armour at fairly close range and therefore it would seem they were not capable of penetrating that armour. The greatest asset of the crossbow was its stunning impact, though it could severely maim when it found a chink in plate armour or was used against mail at close range.

By the second half of the fifteenth century the arbalest was so complicated and expensive that it was frequently used by the younger sons of knights, who were attended by a retainer carrying a pavise. Such men do not appear to have worn much – if any – armour, apart from a helmet. The Swiss in particular employed large numbers of crossbowmen as light troops to shield the approach of their columns of pikemen, and the main role of crossbowmen throughout the 1300–1500 period was to harry and shake the main battle line.

The Longbow

The stave of the English longbow was traditionally made from yew but so great was the demand that only the best

archers were equipped with yew staves; hazel, ash and elm
being used for the others. In length the stave varied from
just under 6 ft. to 6 ft. 4 in., length perhaps being influenced
by the part of the country. The men of Cheshire and Cornwall, for example, were particularly noted for their archery,
and the latter are stated to have used longer arrows than
most, suggesting a stronger pull. The stave had a diameter
of about $1\frac{1}{2}$ in. at the centre, tapering to less than 1 in. at the
ends. A yarn lashing was applied to the middle for about
12 in. to reinforce the wood and provide a hand grip. At the
two ends were notches, sometimes grooved horn tips, to
take the loops of the bowstring. The bowstring itself was of
flax or linen and because of its susceptibility to damp was
only fitted immediately before action commenced. Each
archer usually carried two spare strings. The string was
waxed with beeswax to ensure a quick release of the arrow.

The arrows were made of birch, ash and even oak, the
first being the most popular. They were divided into two
types: lightweight flight arrows and heavy sheaf arrows, the
latter being an armour-piercing version for close range
work. Length varied from 27 to 37 in. The heads, or piles,
were designed to punch their way through armour and were
of steel, about 2 in. long and $\frac{3}{8}$ in. wide at the base, with a
very sharp point to concentrate the force of the blow. In
section they were square, triangular or even diamond, and
no broader than the shaft. They were fixed to the shaft by
socket and rivet.

Mail was no defence against sheaf arrows, which occasionally penetrated plate armour if they obtained a square
hit at close range. Gerald de Barri tells in his chronicle of
arrows from Welsh longbows seen by himself in the oak
door at Abergavenny Castle in the late twelfth century.
They had pierced the oak, which was two inches thick, and
their heads protruded an inch clear of the door on the inside.
In another part of the chronicle he tells of an arrow penetrating the skirt of a hauberk, the gambeson beneath it, the
mail hose beneath that, through the wearer's leg and out

through the hose the other side to pin the man's leg to the saddle. Because of their trajectory flight arrows were mainly ineffectual against knights and lacked the stunning effect of crossbow bolts.

Goose feathers were used to flight the arrows, fixed to the shaft by pitch and silk thread and set at right angles so as to impart spin. They had to be positioned very carefully to enable them to pass over the stave without effect and this was achieved by setting one feather straight and two others at an angle of about 30 degrees to the shaft. The straight feather had to be set away from the stave when placing it on the string and coloured cock feathers were used for this flight to enable the archer to identify that flight instantaneously. The shaft was notched and lashed above the feathers to fit over the string.

When fitted to the bow the arrow always passed on the right side of the stave and the string was pulled back by the first three fingers, the arrow being held between the second and first. A pull of somewhat over 80 lb. was required and a leather glove was worn on the right hand to protect the fingers. A leather or horn bracer was strapped to the inside of the left forearm to protect it from the slap of the released string. The string had to be drawn back to the ear to obtain the maximum range of about 300 yards. (Eighteenth and nineteenth century tests did achieve 308, 310 and 340 yd., but these ranges were exceptional). A more effective range was about 200 yd., while sheaf arrows would not have been fired at more than 80 to 100 yards. Five aimed shafts could be fired in a minute, but it was possible for a good archer to fire up to twelve unaimed shafts in the same time. Usually one or two dozen arrows were carried in the belt or, less often, in a simple quiver. When drawn up for battle four dozen arrows were usually placed before each archer, with more available from the baggage wagons in the rear, although the archers generally preferred to retrieve those which had fallen close to their front, i.e. the more telling sheaf arrows.

The Short Bow

Other nationalities employed bowmen as light troops, particularly from the peasant levy, to skirmish ahead of the main battle line or to guard the flanks, but these were armed with the short bow. There is very little information available on these bows, which seem to have been about 4 ft. long and either of elm or yew, shaped like the longbow, or composite staves of horn, leather and wood. The bowstring was drawn back only to the chest. All this points to a lesser range and penetration power. Exact figures cannot be given but, using the Eastern composite bow as a guide, it is likely that a 24 in. arrow could be fired up to 250 yd., with an effective range of about 100 yards.

The Sling

The sling was still in use as a weapon in the early fourteenth century but seems to have declined in importance after about 1325 and fallen from use by mid-century. Slingers could hurl a lead bullet with considerable accuracy and in rapid volleys, creating a hail of missiles which made them extremely useful as skirmishers before the main battle commenced. Maximum range was greater than the short bow but less than that of the longbow, making it about 275 yards. Slingers played no part in the main battle, lacking the weapons and training for such fighting. They were also of great value at sieges, where scores of thousands of missiles might be fired, for stones or lead bullets were plentiful and cheap whereas in 1300 crossbow bolts cost the equivalent of 5p each. The disadvantage, as with the longbow, was that a high degree of skill was required for slingers to be really effective and regular practice was therefore vital, usually beginning in boyhood.

A staff sling was sometimes used to hurl larger projectiles, the staff about 4 ft. long, and this weapon was capable of throwing a stone ball rather larger than a cricket ball. Occasionally bottles of quicklime were thrown from these slings, the lime forming a cloud of choking, blinding dust. During siege and naval warfare the staff sling was also used to hurl inflammable materials.

Cannon

We know from manuscripts belonging to the city of Ghent that some form of ordnance existed as early as 1313; that in 1324 cannon were being used at the siege of Metz; and that in 1326 Florence ordered a delivery of iron balls and brass cannon for the defence of the city. The first known illustrations of ordnance also occur in 1326 and 1327. Both show a vase-shaped cast brass cannon lying on a trestle table (probably bound to it, in fact) and being fired by the application of a hot iron to a touch hole on the upper surface. The French called these guns *pots de fer*, the Italians *vasi*; both names referring to the shape. The illustrations are probably exaggerated and it is likely that the bulbous end was only slightly swollen, to give greater strength to the part where the charge was exploded. A surviving cannon of this type, found in Sweden, is 18 in. long, and from documents we know that a French fleet raiding Southampton in 1338 carried a *pot de fer* which weighed 25 pounds. Also on board were 3 lb. of gunpowder and 48 projectiles, which gives some idea of the charge used.

However, the most important part of these illustrations is the missile emerging from the gun; a heavy iron arrow with brass flights, the charge presumably being wadded and the end of the arrow probably wrapped with leather to obtain a tight fit. Such a weapon was an anti-personnel one – making the *vasi* little more than a gunpowder powered crossbow – whereas those at Florence and Metz fired balls and, judging from illustrations in later fourteenth century manuscripts, would probably have been large, squat and rather clumsy pieces of the mortar type. Thus from the

Breech-loading bronze gun from Turkey, dated 1464, the screw-on chamber similar to that of the great Flemish bombard *Dulle Griete*. Weight of stone shot, six cwt.

beginning there were two distinct types of ordnance, although it was to be more than a century before a field gun capable of outdistancing the longbow and crossbow would be developed.

These early cannon could be cast in brass or made of wrought iron, for the art of casting iron guns was not acquired until the 1540s. Brass casting was a well developed process by the fourteenth century, but making cannon of wrought iron was a complicated and not always hundred per-cent successful business. Red-hot wrought iron bars were placed round a wooden core and held in position by the shrinking on of between two and six white hot hoops. (Later more hoops were used, covering the entire surface.) The whole assembly was then placed in a fire hot enough to fuse the iron together and burn out the core. Molten lead was used to fill any cracks. From this simple tube two types of cannon could be made; muzzle loading or breech loading. Most of the early wrought iron cannon were quite small and one end of the tube could quite easily be closed by an iron chamber holding a powder charge, held in place by a wedge between it and a barrier at the rear of the gun. These chambers were bottle-shaped, with an opening which aligned with the breech and a touch hole for firing the charge. Thus we read in the inventory for the king's vessels which fought at Sluys in 1340, 'un canon de fer ov ii chambers, un autre de brass ove une chamber, iii canons de fer of v chambres, un handgonne . . .' and so on. The advantage of having several chambers for a gun was that a fairly high rate of fire could be achieved.

Larger wrought-iron guns were soon developed and by the last quarter of the fourteenth century guns capable of firing balls weighing 200 lb. were in use. The chambers of such large guns were rather unwieldy and therefore many of these larger guns would have been muzzle-loaders, with the breech end blocked by a plug, held in place by the framework built round the gun on the ground. However, just as many remained breech loaders, such as the bombards used by the English at Mont St Michel in 1424, which had a chamber 3 ft. long, and the great Flemish bombard called Dulle Griete of 1430 which fired a shot with a diameter of 25 inches. The chamber of this last gun screwed on to the barrel. (Wrought-iron guns of this period were called bombards from the Greek word *bombos*, meaning a loud humming noise like a bee.)

Iron balls were used initially but their cost and weight were disadvantages as guns became larger and stone balls were used instead for the larger guns. These had the advantage of being lighter and required a smaller charge of powder, thus reducing the danger of an explosion in the wrong direction, but were less effective because sometimes the stones shattered on impact with fortifications. Some of the guns were designed to throw their projectiles over the defences rather than attempting to batter them down, and in this case the splinters from a shattering stone ball would have been quite effective as an anti-personnel weapon. The gunpowder used for the guns was usually mixed on the spot because it tended to separate into the various ingredients during transportation, and occasionally exploded. Loading the charge was also a delicate matter, for if rammed in too tightly the powder would not ignite instantaneously throughout, but if packed too loosely it might fail to ignite all the powder.

There were no gun carriages in the fourteenth century and the guns were simply secured to wooden beams by ropes or iron straps, or placed on the ground and lashed to wooden frames known as telaria which were erected on each side of it, the breech end being butted against a wooden barrier secured by stakes driven into the ground. They were transported from site to site on ponderous carriages with iron-shod wheels. By the end of the century the guns often had an eye on either side of the upper surface at the point of balance to facilitate lifting into position by means of sheer-legs, ropes and pulleys. Such cranes and static mountings remained in use for the larger guns until the sixteenth century.

In the 1450s gunpowder was granulated to make it more stable, the granules being glazed to resist damp. This was a great improvement but only the smaller, cast guns were strong enough to withstand its force and therefore cannon became divided into the large calibre, stone-throwing siege pieces of wrought iron, using the ordinary powder, and the long but small calibre cast guns using iron shot and granulated powder. The latter were more mobile and were now being used in the field. They could at last outrange the long-bow but were not yet established as an important weapon because of the lack of an effective gun carriage: at this date they were usually strapped to wooden sledges and dragged across the ground.

Some heavier bombards of the mortar type appear to have been mounted on carriages since at least the 1450s, but these could not have been much more than beams into which the bombard was sunk and fastened by straps, with an axle and two crude and clumsy solid wooden wheels. Such a carriage was quite adequate for transporting a gun from one siege to another, but not advanced enough for field artillery. The French had wheeled guns by 1461 but these do not appear to have been used as field artillery either.

Bronze was in general use throughout Europe for cast guns by the 1440s and during the second half of the century many beautiful long guns were cast in bronze. By the turn of the century they had largely superseded the wrought-iron gun. About 1470 these guns began to be cast with small cylindrical blocks at each side and a little in front of the point of balance. These were called trunnions and enabled the gun to be placed on an open framework carriage, acting as pivots to allow the gun to be elevated or depressed. The breech end was supported by a pin between the sides of the carriage, the pin fitting into any pair of a series of holes to alter the elevation, though some of the larger guns employed a chock between the breech and the carriage. The carriage was furnished with an axle and two spoked wheels, the latter shod with iron. There are no contemporary accounts to show how these carriages were moved but at Flodden Field in 1513 the Scottish guns on wheeled carriages were pulled by a horse and 16 oxen, or by a horse and 8 oxen. Thirteen carts carried 52 barrels of powder between them and 28 pack horses carried the projectiles in panniers. The first really mobile field artillery accompanied Charles VIII on his invasion of Italy in 1494 and Fornovo in 1495 was probably the first battle where field artillery played a really effective part.

Case shot is first recorded as early as 1410 and case, canister and grape shot appear to have been common by mid-century. (The early case shot, called langridge, had been loaded loose.) These projectiles were introduced to increase the effectiveness of the small cannon against personnel. Canister consisted of a container filled with ball, case shot a container filled with nails, scrap iron and small stones,

Breech-loading peterara of forged iron with chamber missing. *c.* 1460–1470: carriage is modern.

and grape a bag packed with small round shot. By the late fifteenth century an effective range for cannon would seem to have been 200 yd., with a maximum range of from 350 to 500 yd., the latter for the cast guns with long barrels to increase velocity. Rate of fire would not have exceeded

15-inch forged bombard of the early fifteenth century on a modern carriage. Weight of stone-shot, 160 pounds.

about four rounds an hour, unless using extra chambers in the case of breech loaders.

Mention was made earlier of the development of anti-personnel ordnance at an early stage; i.e. the *vasi* firing arrows. The next mention of anti-personnel ordnance occurs in the accounts of Bruges in 1339 when a weapon called the ribauldequin is described as being several cannon (calibre would probably range from 1–3 in. for these cannon) clamped together on a wooden platform so that a cannoneer could fire them simultaneously with a sweep of his slow match: slow match – cord soaked in saltpetre and sulphur – was introduced about the middle of the fourteenth century. The platform had wheels, thus forming the first gun carriage, and the gunner was often protected by a mantling attached to the platform – the first gun shield. This weapon is sometimes referred to as a cart of war and was loaded with a large number of small round shot. Its great disadvantage was the length of time needed to reload, but it must have provided an awesome threat, as at the siege of Tournai in 1340 when ribauldequins were placed so as to command the city gates. In 1345 Edward III ordered 100 ribauldequins to be constructed for his invasion of France and they appear to have been used at the siege of Calais to prevent the breakthrough of a relieving force. In 1387 an exceptional ribauldequin with 144 handgun barrels was made, the barrels grouped in 'batteries' of 12 so that 12 salvoes of 12 balls could be fired without reloading. The weapon remained popular throughout the period with which we are concerned, the Scottish Parliament in 1456 and again in 1471 ordering the construction of carts of war each having two guns, and each with two chambers.

Handguns

The first mention of handguns occurs in the Sluys inventory mentioned earlier, but the next occurrence is not until 1364 when Perugia in Italy purchased 500 handguns. The development of the handgun is unlikely to have lagged behind that of the cannon and it is probable therefore that handguns were in use during the first half of the fourteenth century but did not become widespread until about 1360, by which time slow match would have made the handgunner more mobile. (Prior to the invention of slow match, gunpowder was ignited with hot iron or wire, which meant staying close to a fire!) They were first used in Germany in 1381, in France and England in 1386.

The first handguns were just small cannon attached to a wooden shaft by a socket, weighed about 10 lb. and fired a lead bullet. The shaft was tucked under the arm with the butt resting on the ground to take the recoil, with the result that such weapons could only be fired at a high trajectory. They were therefore slow to load and inaccurate in firing, and their inferiority to existing missile weapons must have retarded their development and popularity.

Towards the end of the century the handgun became less cumbersome, with a barrel about 8 in. long and very similar in shape to that of a modern pistol, except that the calibre was about 1 inch. It was now usually fixed to a short wooden stock, although some were cast in one piece with a metal handle, but surviving examples have a lug on the underside which could be hooked over a wall to check the recoil, and this indicates that at this date the handgun was designed primarily for the defence of fortifications. This type of handgun remained in general use until at least 1450.

In the early fifteenth century the rear end of the stock on some handguns was bent downwards slightly so that it could be rested against the chest, and a Z-shaped lever called the serpentine was fixed to the side of the shaft to enable the gun to be fired mechanically. The upper arm of this lever held the match over the touch hole and by pressing up the rear arm the glowing match was pushed into the hole. These guns could be aimed more accurately but were still not very effective even at short range unless fired in volleys.

During the middle part of the century the stock was altered so that it could be held against the shoulder and the serpentine was replaced by a matchlock mechanism which was spring-loaded and prevented the match swinging down to fire the gun accidentally. These locks were let into the side of the stock and covered by a metal plate to protect them. The matchlock originated in Germany and perhaps because of the hooked 'hammer' was called a hakenbüsche – hookgun – which became 'arquebuse' in France and 'arcebuse' or 'harcebus' in England.

These improved weapons became more widely used than the earlier firearms and many companies of men were trained in their use, mainly Germans in the mid-century, but later men of other nations. When Edward IV landed at Ravenspur from Flushing in 1471 to claim the English crown he was accompanied by a corps of 320 Flemish handgunners, and in 1487 2,000 harcebusiers were killed at the battle of Stoke fighting for the Earl of Lincoln against Henry VII.

A primitive form of pistol, just a smaller version of the matchlock, was used by some cavalry after the 1450s and in the 1490s the first mounted arquebusiers were used by the Condottiero Camillo Vitelli. These were apparently light cavalrymen, and were used as skirmishers both when mounted and on foot. (Cavalry firearms were not really effective or practical until the invention of the wheel-lock in Germany in 1517.)

The handgun of the late fifteenth century had the advantage of being easy to use once a man had been trained; anyone could be trained in a few weeks and handgunners did not need great strength and constant practice as did the longbowman. It also had a penetrative power equal to that of the longbow, was very effective at close range in volleys, and the arquebusier could carry far more shots than an archer could carry arrows. Its disadvantages were that it was slow to load, a maximum of perhaps eight shots an hour before 1500, misfires were frequent, and it was inaccurate and ineffective if fired singly. Maximum range may have been as much as 400 yd., but the effective range would have been about 200 yd. and accurate range considerably less.

CHAPTER FOUR

Tactics

OF all the aspects of medieval warfare to undergo radical
change during the 1300–1500 period, tactics was the one to
be the most drastically revolutionized. The supremacy of
the armoured horseman over infantry had been finally
established at the battle of Hastings in 1066 and for the next
two-and-a-half centuries feudal cavalry dominated the
battlefields of Europe, but during the fourteenth and
fifteenth centuries new weapons and new tactics created an
infantry arm capable of defeating cavalry on the open
battlefield.

We will deal with these developments in detail later; first
let us take a look at the tactics commonly employed
throughout Europe in the first half of the fourteenth
century, and which remained in use throughout the fourteenth and most of the fifteenth centuries in many parts of
Europe. It is still a popular conception that medieval armies
were unskilled, undisciplined mobs, led by men with no
knowledge of tactics, and that battles were little more than
free-for-alls in which the strongest individuals survived and
the army with the most cavalry emerged victorious. I hope

to show that, in the light of recent studies, this is a misconception.

The infantry in particular is written off by many authors as an ill-armed, undisciplined rabble, of no use except for menial tasks in the camp or at a siege, yet history records a far different story: at Hastings the Anglo-Saxon infantry was defeated because it was unsupported by cavalry, but the Norman cavalry was victorious only because the English shield wall was first broken by the archers of the supporting infantry. It seems to me that much of the confusion stems from a failure to recognise the distinctive types of infantry which existed during the eleventh to fourteenth centuries, and which are described fully in the chapters on organisation, weapons and armour. Contemporary manuscripts portray ordinary foot soldiers uniformly equipped and quite heavily armoured, indicating they played a far more important role than the manuscripts themselves imply. These were the mercenaries, the crossbowmen and spearmen. However, it is usually believed also that the unarmoured and poorly armed rabble of the feudal levy was totally at the mercy of the cavalry. So it was in defeat, as were the mercenaries, but in mêlées these light troops could create such havoc amongst the horses that trappers had to be used, while the knights were forced to wear complex leg armour to protect their lower limbs from the long knives, axes and polearms of the peasants.

The main problem seems to have been not the fighting quality of the troops, but the inability to maintain discipline over them once battle commenced, for loyalties within an army were widely divided, the nobles were jealous of each other and arrogant towards the infantry, and even kings could not control such internally divided armies. Because of this there is a great deal of truth in the belief that after the first charge a battle degenerated into a series of individual combats in which even the leaders took part. The nobles were fiercely proud and could rarely be prevailed upon to follow a set of detailed orders. If a chance occurred to strike the enemy before their rivals, the commander's plan would be forgotten, and they would lead their command straight for the enemy, frequently running blindly into ditches, bogs or hedges. This made it difficult to launch a coordinated attack, or even to withhold a reserve, for every lord wished to be in the front line and regarded it as a slur on his honour to be held out of the main action.

Nevertheless, medieval commanders must have employed some degree of drill and tactics to bring their armies into contact with each other, although there is little definite information available concerning such matters. Yet it is obvious that if a noble had to marshal and move a body of troops from A to B he would soon invent sufficient 'drill' to do so and also devise formations which would enable them to take the offensive or defensive. The commander of several such bodies would of necessity invent basic tactics to combine them in a general plan of battle, making the most of their various qualities. Experience would create better tactics, and there was plenty of opportunity for experience in the Middle Ages.

It is true that in the fourteenth century most armies still had a large proportion of feudal levies, and that the leaders were elected for their territorial possessions rather than their military skill, but the troops were accustomed to handling their weapons and were occasionally mustered, so must have had some basic organisation, while the men who commanded them were trained fighting men even if they were not outstanding military leaders. From the age of seven until early adolescence they served as pages to their liege lord, followed by seven to eight years as a squire, all the time gaining experience of weapons, armour, horses and battle; for no squire could become a knight until 'qualified' in these skills. In addition the ability to command was expected of *all* the nobility, for all were expected to command their own retinues initially.

We know from accounts of medieval battles that from the late eleventh century the leaders were often careful to secure their flanks by the use of natural obstacles, take up defensive positions on high ground fronted by some form of natural barrier, and hold a force in reserve, while night surprises and ambushes were favourite devices. These facts, combined with the high standard of siege warfare, indicate that medieval warfare was not such a haphazard affair as we are often led to believe, and that many commanders of European armies had read the surviving military writings of the Romans and some had studied these methods in use whilst on crusade.

When the European chivalry first met the Saracens they crushed them with their massively heavy charges, but the Saracens soon learnt to avoid such charges and the knights found themselves powerless against a far more mobile enemy who could bombard them with arrows without ever being brought to a mêlée. Their answer was to develop an infantry arm of bowmen to counter the Saracen arrows and heavy infantry to provide shelter for the cavalry when necessary: a combination of shock and missile troops exactly as used at Hastings and as laid down in the Roman military writings still extant and put into application by the Byzantine armies since at least the fourth century A.D.

Both on the march and on the battlefield these infantry were placed between the knights and the enemy, the cavalry only charging out at the decisive moment. The infantry were incapable of successful offensive action on their own and could not survive against repeated cavalry and missile attacks without the support of cavalry. On the other hand the cavalry were usually defeated if their first charge was repulsed and they had no infantry behind which to rally.

At Jaffa in 1191 we hear for the first time of a tactic which later occurs throughout Europe. Richard I of England had a force of 2,000 infantry, mostly Italians and including 400 crossbowmen, and fifty knights with ten horses. He arranged his infantry in a line behind a row of tent pegs to break up any enemy cavalry charges, each crossbowman supported by a spearman and both sheltering behind the

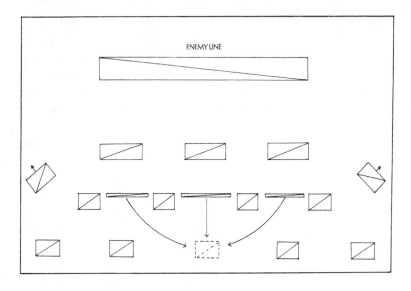

Order of battle for Byzantine cavalry. (After Oman).

spearman's large shield, which had its point set in the ground so as to form a shield wall. The crossbowmen were able to fire at any attackers, while the Saracens were prevented from charging the crossbowmen by the levelled spears. The few cavalry were held back to make a charge at a decisive moment. (In fact the Saracens refused to attack such a strong line and Richard took the offensive.) Richard may have been responsible for this idea, but it may already have been standard Italian practice, for in 1259 and 1260 the laws of Florence describe the city's infantry as being divided into companies of spearmen equipped with large shields and companies of crossbowmen and archers. On the march the shields were carried on mules and the companies were only mixed immediately before a battle.

It is now believed that the Crusaders also adopted the Byzantine cavalry tactic of charging in successive waves. Byzantine cavalry were drawn up in three main lines: the first of three banda of 450 men; the second of four half-banda of about 225 men, stationed to cover the ends and intervals of the first line; and the third line of two half-banda to the rear of the second line's flanks. The gaps between the banda of the second line were bridged by sections of another bandon, which retired to form the centre of the third line, thus creating gaps for the first line to withdraw through if necessary. In addition there were two half-banda on each flank to prevent outflanking moves by the enemy (see diagram). Such an arrangement allowed up to five successive charges, and it is obvious from this that by the tenth century the Byzantines understood the most important factor of cavalry battles; the side with the last reserve must win.

Feudal chivalry was not capable of such intricate manoeuvring but the Crusaders did divide their cavalry into several squadrons, six being a common number. These were brigaded into three Battles and drawn up in two lines, or in echelon if the front was cramped. Successive charges were made by the Battles and their individual squadrons against different parts of the enemy line, each squadron rallying back behind the line of spearmen, who were in turn supported by the archers and crossbowmen; a far different picture from the one usually painted.

So here we have the basic tactics for most European cavalry and infantry which dominated the battlefields during the early fourteenth century; successive waves of cavalry supported by spearmen and missile men, with the heavy cavalry as the decisive arm, for back in Europe the chivalry was no longer faced by light, mobile archers, nor did an enemy stand off and bombard them with missiles, and consequently the infantry remained inferior in numbers and role.

Reducing warfare to its simplest level we can see that there are only two ways of defeating an enemy: shock tactics involving a hand-to-hand mêlée which attempts to break the enemy by the violence and moral effect of the charge; or the use of missiles to destroy the enemy before he can come to close quarters, or to drive him from the field if he assumes a passive defensive position. These two methods may be combined; as they were at Hastings, where missiles were used to break the English shield wall and allow the cavalry to charge through the breaks; but until the four-teenth century the heavy cavalry and shock tactics remained predominant, mainly because the bow was a short-range weapon ineffective against both mail and padded clothing, while the crossbow was slow to load and also lacked penetrative power. The simple longbow with its rapid rate of fire and great penetrative power altered all this drastically during the first half of the fourteenth century.

The English Longbow

The origin of the longbow is obscure and many sources state that its use was at first restricted to South Wales, where the English discovered its effectiveness during the Welsh Wars. Other sources name Sherwood, the Chilterns and the Sussex Weald as areas in which the longbow was in common use before the fourteenth century, and certainly in the campaign of 1282 Edward I was employing a small number of English archers as well as English and Gascon crossbowmen: 240,000 bolts were used, compared with 16,000 arrows.

In the ensuing years Edward used more and more archers in preference to crossbows: in 1282 there were 850 cross-bowmen in his army; in 1289 105; in 1292 only 70; and in the next century the use of the crossbow declined even further in English armies. A classical example of the com-bination of missile in the form of the longbow and shock in the shape of cavalry occurred at Orewin Bridge in 1282. The Welsh, mainly spearmen, had taken up a position on the forward slope of a hill overlooking the bridge but just beyond bowshot, and any attempt to force a crossing by infantry would have enabled them to engage as much of the

English force at close quarters as they chose, with the remainder unable to advance in support. However, at dawn the next day English infantry crossed the river upstream by an unguarded ford and attacked the Welsh in the flank. The Welsh retired to make a stand on the hilltop where, exactly as at Hastings, their ranks were broken by a hail of arrows before the cavalry charged home.

Edward was not slow to appreciate the value of the longbow and he raised and trained a large corps of archers for the later campaigns in North Wales, many of them coming from the border county of Shropshire. In 1298 he took them to Scotland and at Falkirk defeated 10,000 Scottish infantry and 200 knights with 2,500 knights and 12,500 Welsh, Cheshire and Lancashire infantry.

Scottish armies of that time consisted mainly of infantry armed with 12-ft. spears, for the Highlanders with their targe and broadsword took little part in the wars, and therefore the tactics used in Wales were able to be repeated successfully. The Scots under Wallace were positioned on the forward slope of a hill, their front covered by a marsh, and formed in four great schiltrons or hedgehogs of spearmen, with a few archers in the intervals and the 200 knights to the rear. It was impossible to cross the marsh so Edward's two flank Battles went round the ends, the Main Battle under Edward following to the right. The Scottish archers were soon ridden down and the Scottish knights fled, but the English cavalry could not break the schiltrons and many horses and knights were killed in a first wild rush before Edward arrived and put a stop to such foolishness. He ordered forward the archers, and the spearmen died by the hundred, unable to either advance or retreat because of the cavalry poised to strike. Gaps soon began to appear in the hedges, the cavalry went in, and the spearmen were annihilated. The disaster at Bannockburn in 1314, when 23,000 men under Edward II were defeated by 10,000 Scots under Bruce, was a direct result of the cavalry trying to go it alone.

Edward II had allowed the training of longbowmen to

lapse during his reign but when Edward III began his reign in 1327 at the age of 15 he immediately began raising and training longbowmen again and the victories of Dupplin in 1332 and Halidon Hill in 1333 in Scotland were a result of the judicious mixing of the infantry and cavalry arms. At Dupplin 500 English knights and between 1,500 and 2,000 hired archers faced a Scottish army of about 10,000. The English took position on a hill with the knights dismounted in the centre, apart from a small mounted reserve, and the archers on the flanks, slightly forward so as to sweep the front with their fire. The Scottish spearmen attacked in three columns, all aimed at the men-at-arms but, their attack weakened by the hail of arrows from the flanks, were halted by the thin line. Once halted the great columns became almost useless and, hemmed in by the archers on their flanks, gradually became more and more jammed into the centre until the whole force was virtually wiped out, the English reserve cutting down any who broke away from the rear. The following year Edward defeated the Scots at Halidon Hill using dismounted men-at-arms in support of archers, but remounted his cavalry to charge and break the enemy when their advance faltered in face of the arrows. These tactics were used successfully against the Scots throughout the fifteenth and sixteenth centuries, the Scots unable to train a corps of longbowmen with which to reply.

These battles set the pattern for English tactics against the French in the Hundred Years War. Edward realised that it would be impossible to fight the French chivalry in conventional cavalry-versus-cavalry battles because of the vast numerical superiority of the French, and he therefore dismounted his men-at-arms and supported them with archers, the flanks of the line always secured by natural obstacles. Thus at Crécy he drew up his forces in what was to become the standard English battle line: two dismounted Battles of men-at-arms with the archers in wedge-shaped blocks, known as *en herse*, at the ends of the line and between the two Battles. The third Battle and its archers was held as a

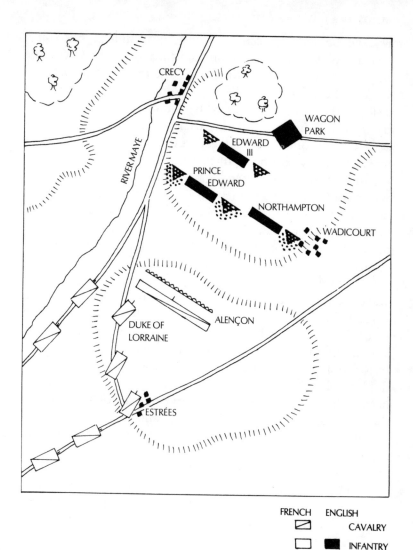

CRECY

WAGON PARK

EDWARD III

PRINCE EDWARD

NORTHAMPTON

WADICOURT

RIVER MAYE

ALENÇON

DUKE OF LORRAINE

ESTRÉES

FRENCH	ENGLISH	
▱		CAVALRY
▢	◼	INFANTRY
ᴧᴧᴧ	ᴧᴧᴧ	ARCHERS
∴∵∴		PIT FALLS

Crécy, 1346. At Crécy Edward III drew up his forces in what was to become the standard order of battle used by English armies throughout the Hundred Years War.

reserve behind the centre, ready to mount if necessary. Terrain played a vital part in English tactics. At Crécy the English right rested on the River Maye and the Forest of Crécy; the left on the village of Wadicourt, woodland and a slope; the front was covered by the slope of a hill, the rear by a wood. In addition the archers dug many one-foot-square holes, one foot deep, across their front to prevent the enemy cavalry closing with them.

Philip had 35,000 men against the English 10,000, of whom only 1,141 were men-at-arms, but his command was unruly with such distinguished leaders as the king of Bohemia and Majorca, and the Duke of Savoy only nominally under his command. His army arrived in a long strung-out column in the late afternoon, and he therefore ordered a halt for the night, but those to the rear continued to press forward and the vanguard was forced to advance on the English line. The only infantry with the vanguard were 5,000 Genoese crossbowmen. They were sent forward to soften up the English line, but their crossbows were inferior in accuracy and rate of fire to the longbow and it is doubtful if any of them had time to fire more than once before they were overwhelmed by the hail of shafts from the English archers. Bewildered and suffering heavy casualties, the Genoese fell back in disorder and the French chivalry, impatient at this display, rode through and over the survivors to charge the English.

Seeing the traps before the archers, and because they considered it beneath their dignity to offer battle to infantry – who were after all only peasants and had no ransom value, the French chivalry crowded in on the centre to attack the men-at-arms. The archers, having no aim in battle beyond the desire to win, committed the unthinkable atrocity of aiming at the horses and caused great damage to the French advance, hundreds of horses being shot down and many knights injured or trapped by their frenzied horses. Yet the longbow alone did not decide this battle, for fifteen separate charges were made by the cavalry as fresh forces arrived on the field, and in some of these there was desperate hand-to-hand fighting with the English men-at-arms, although the French did not at any one time get through in sufficient numbers to make a serious impression. At nightfall the French withdrew, having lost a third of their number.

The longbow had proved so devastating because, until it was superseded by efficient handguns and cannon in the middle of the fifteenth century, it had a greater penetration power than any other weapon and a rapidity of fire which enabled a skilled bowman to fire a dozen unaimed arrows a minute. Advancing uphill across uneven ground and carrying a heavily armoured knight, a horse might cover about a hundred yards in a minute. Therefore the French cavalry must have been in range of the archers for three minutes before closing to mêlée. Every archer could have fired 36 arrows, although as they only had about 48 arrows each they probably fired about 30, the others being reserved for aimed shots at close range – capable of piercing mail. At Crécy there were 5,500 archers and during the French advances they must have fired at least thirty volleys of 5,500 arrows – 150,000 arrows, perhaps more since they would have retrieved some arrows between charges. These massive volleys must have darkened the sky and the accompanying howl and drone of arrows and bowstrings must have demoralised an army encountering the weapon for the first time. Certainly the volleys caused havoc amongst the horses and in future battles occasionally caused even the most experienced warriors to glance fearfully upwards, to receive an arrow in the face, as did Prince Harry, later Henry V, at Shrewsbury.

Edward III had another advantage over the French: he fought to kill. The feudal cavalry which formed the bulk of the French armies, and indeed most European armies of this period, still regarded the battlefield as an extension of the tournament, a place where glory and fortunes could be won, and ransom was the main objective. This explains the French attitude at Crécy, where they ignored the yeomen archers entirely, and after the battle refused to accept that the archers had decided the day, blaming their defeat on the fact that the English men-at-arms had fought dismounted. Therefore, when the two sides met again at Poitiers in 1356 the French dismounted two-thirds of their cavalry.

At Poitiers the English drew up in their usual line but, because the right flank could not be rested on any natural obstacle, trenches were dug and the wagons parked here to form a barrier against a cavalry charge. Their front was to some extent protected by vineyards on the slope of the hill. The French sent in two forlorn hopes of 250 mounted men-at-arms backed by crossbowmen and spearmen to shake the English line, but these were easily repulsed. Then the first of the lines of dismounted men-at-arms began to advance. The vineyards were no great obstacle, but the line had to advance uphill for about a kilometre and they arrived hot and tired. The longbowmen were not numerous enough in this battle to prevent the enemy closing, although they must have fired at least 80,000 arrows and inflicted some casualties on the French during the advance, and the first French line was principally defeated by the men-at-arms. The archers were now out of arrows and Edward had been forced to commit almost all his reserve Battle to hold the left. However, for some reason the second French line did not advance, but joined the retreating first line. King John of France therefore dismounted his third line and began to advance, but they too had over a kilometre to cover and Edward seized the initiative by mounting his men and charging down on the French, whose horses were now far to the rear. At the same time he sent his small cavalry reserve in a right hook at the French rear and after a fierce struggle the French line broke and fled, leaving their king and 2,000 knights prisoner.

The military disgrace of Poitiers was directly responsible for the widespread disorder which now spread through France. In 1358 came the bloody atrocities of the peasant uprisings, and here lies the main reason why the longbow was never adopted by the French, or indeed any other

European country. The longbow required a pull of about eighty pounds to fire effectively and this meant it was not possible to hold and aim. Aiming had to be almost unconscious; a steady pull, quick aim and swift release. To achieve this a man needed constant practice, and therefore needed to have his own bow and arrows, not weapons issued from an arsenal in times of crisis. Because of the wide gulf between the French chivalry and the peasantry the French ruling classes did not dare so arm the peasantry.

The Black Prince died in 1376, Edward III in 1377 and the tide at last began to turn in favour of the French. Bertrand du Guesclin was made Constable of France and he realised that to recapture the lost territories he need only control the key castles. Using almost exclusively an army of professionals recruited from the Free Companies, du Guesclin and his successors fought a war of harassment, ambushes, and sieges. He refused to be drawn into open battle and kept the chivalry sulking in their castles.

Yet at Agincourt in 1415 the French chivalry showed that it had learnt nothing from du Guesclin's successes. The French had defeated a Flemish army of infantry at Roosebeke in 1382 with a frontal assault by dismounted men-at-arms, supported by simultaneous flank attacks by cavalry. These tactics had caused the Flemings to bunch helplessly on the centre, where they were slaughtered. The French decided to employ similar tactics at Agincourt, where they had about 30,000 men against 6,000 English, 5,000 of whom were archers. But the French had refused to see that Agincourt was different from Roosebeke, for in their usual fashion the English had made sure their flanks were protected by thick woods, although they were so few in number that they could form only a single line with no reserve. And yet the French line up was basically sound: cavalry, guns and crossbowmen on the flanks to support the advance of two lines of dismounted men-at-arms in the centre, with a third line of mounted men-at-arms for the pursuit. The blame, as always, must lie on the attitude of the French

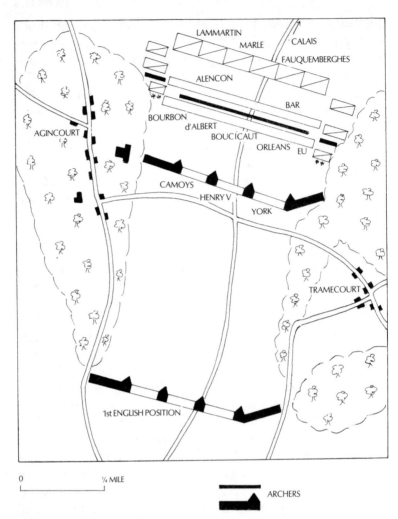

LAMMARTIN

MARLE

CALAIS

FAUQUEMBERGHES

ALENCON

BAR

BOURBON
d'ALBERT
BOUCICAUT
ORLEANS EU

AGINCOURT

CAMOYS
HENRY V
YORK

TRAMECOURT

1st ENGLISH POSITION

0   ¼ MILE

ARCHERS

Agincourt, 1415.

nobles, so many of whom insisted on crowding into the
front line that it became so extended that the guns could not
fire and many of the cavalry on the flanks were unable to
squeeze through to charge the flanking archers. Those
whose horses were not shot from under them were halted
by the sharpened stakes set before the archers.

Armour was much heavier than at Poitiers, and the dis-mounted men-at-arms plodding over muddy ground were severely harassed by the archers, arriving at the English line already exhausted. Even so they forced the centre back but because of the cramped situation, with those on the French flanks converging on the centre to escape the point-blank fire from the flanking archers, were unable to wield their weapons effectively and were cut down in their hundreds by the English men-at-arms and the brawny, agile archers, who seized discarded axes, maces and swords, or used their mauls, to batter the French to the ground, where they were despatched by a knife blade through the visor or smothered in the mud and the dead.

The second line struggled determinedly over the churned-up ground but again became cramped in the centre and could not advance past the high barrier of dead and woun-ded in front of the English line. The third French line ignominiously rode away. The French lost 1,600 nobles and knights, 3,000 or more men-at-arms, and untold thousands of infantry, yet the longbow had not prevented them from closing and a major reason for their defeat must surely be the lack of discipline amongst the chivalry.

The successes of the French in the 1430s were not due to a change in tactics but mainly to the inspiration of Joan of Arc, who had led the French forces to attack the English before they could take up their usual impregnable position. Loyalty to the French crown was rekindled and the loss of Burgundy as an ally in 1435 signalled the end of English dominance, for the English were too small a race to hold down a country the size of France on their own. During the uneasy truce in the 1440s the French organised a national army and developed a train of artillery second to none in Europe, and at Formigny in 1450 the longbow at last met its match.

At this battle the English army of about 4,500 men was drawn up on a slope in its usual array but the French, who had slightly more men, did not make their usual assault with men-at-arms. After two hours of skirmishing the French brought forward two culverins which enfiladed the massed archers and began to mow them down in large numbers from beyond bowshot. Some of the archers broke ranks and charged the guns, overrunning them, but the French infantry was now able to charge home and at close quarters made short work of the lightly armoured archers. The culverins were not wheeled, and the French were only able to bring them to bear because the English line remained stationary.

No other country adopted the longbow but English archers fought in many parts of Europe with the Free Companies, and before leaving this weapon it is perhaps best to look at what happened when longbow met longbow. The first such encounter was at the battle of Shrewsbury in 1403 when the rebel forces of the Earl of Northumberland fought Henry IV. The Percy army of 10,000 men was drawn up on a hill with the archers to the fore. The royal army of about 30,000 also had the archers in the front line and the battle opened with the royal archers advancing up the hill. The Percy archers were more numerous and came from Cheshire – famous for its archers. After a shattering exchange of fire the king's archers broke and ran down the hill, followed by the Percy men-at-arms. The royal army was forced back but, because it was much larger, it over-lapped the flanks of the rebels and on the left the Battle under Prince Harry worked round the flank and on to the rear of the force under Hotspur Percy. Hotspur was killed and the rebels broke and fled, but it is important to note that the decision was reached by the men-at-arms, not the archers, and that when both sides had longbowmen the main victims of the arrows were the archers. During the Wars of the Roses the same rule applied and both sides were usually compelled to come to a mêlée as soon as possible.

The Swiss Pike

At the same time that the longbow was rising to prominence another infantry weapon was changing warfare in a
different part of Europe – the polearm. For two-and-a-half
centuries spearmen had been used to support cavalry and
missile men and as early as the thirteenth century Brabanters
armed with 12-ft. spears were hiring themselves out to
France, England and Italy. Such bodies of spearmen were
used by the Scots with varying success against the English,
and in 1302 Flemish infantry defeated the French chivalry at
Courtrai. (The main reason for their success was the boggy
terrain, broken by ditches and hedges, and they were defeated
by the French cavalry at Mons-en-Pevele in 1304 and at
Cassel in 1328.) Because these bodies of spearmen lacked
mobility and speed they were weak on the offensive, and
although strong on the defensive they could not change
front readily: consequently they were invaluable when
used in conjunction with cavalry or missile men, but rarely
decided a battle on their own.

However, in 1291 the forest cantons of Unterwalden,
Schwyz and Uri in Switzerland formed a league and in 1307
the wars of emancipation from the Holy Roman Empire
started and a new infantry force began to emerge which
would ultimately be effective not only in a defensive role
but also in an offensive one. The weapon of the men of the
forest cantons was the halberd and in 1315 at the battle of
Mortgarten it was used with devastating effect against the
feudal cavalry and levies of Duke Leopold I of Austria. The
Austrians were advancing in a long narrow column along a
defile, the knights leading, when suddenly a shower of tree
trunks and rocks descended on them, knocking many into
the lake below on their right. Before they could recover
from their surprise the main body of about 1,500 Swiss
charged into the front of the confused cavalry. The leading
files of knights had no chance to use their lances and were
hewn down in a moment by halberds and Morning Stars.

Because of the mass of about 5,000 infantry to the rear, the knights could not retreat and, trapped within the confines of the defile, could not advance either. Their left flank was continually showered with rocks and logs, their front pressed by the Swiss, and eventually they broke and trampled a way through their own infantry. Hundreds were pushed off the road to drown in the lake below.

At Mortgarten the Swiss were helped by the terrain and the element of surprise, but this was not the case at Laupen in 1339, where they met and defeated a Burgundian army in the open field. During the years between these two dates other cantons had joined the league and the Swiss of the lower Alpine lands had brought to the national army a 'new' weapon – the pike, different from earlier spears in having a longer shaft and a lighter head. This was used in the same manner as the spear for defensive action; the first four ranks levelling their pikes to present an impenetrable wall of points, while those to the rear kept their pikes upright, ready to fill any gaps appearing in the front ranks. Because of its greater length the pike was held differently: the front rank kneeling with the pike held low, the butt resting on the ground behind them; the second rank stooping with the butt held under their right foot; the third rank with the pike held at waist level; and the fourth rank holding the pike at head level. This was the classical Macedonian phalanx and differed little from the hedgehogs of spearmen of the twelfth, thirteenth and fourteenth centuries, but the Swiss were not content merely to assume the defensive. Because they were very lightly armoured – if at all – the columns of pikemen were far more agile than the spearmen, and by constant training and tight discipline developed the ability to manoeuvre swiftly and assume the offensive even against cavalry. For the advance the pike was held horizontally at chest level, the right arm back and the left arm forward, with the pike head pointing slightly downwards.

At Laupen the Swiss formed up in three large columns,

the pikes on the right and in the centre, the halberds of the forest cantons on the left. The Burgundian infantry was trampled down by the pike columns opposing them and driven from the field. The Burgundian chivalry on the left attacked the forest cantons in successive waves and inflicted heavy casualties, the halberds being incapable of keeping them at bay, but when the two victorious pike columns turned to engage them the Burgundian cavalry rode from the field.

At Sempach in 1385 Duke Leopold, taking note of the ineffectiveness of cavalry against pikes at Laupen, dismounted his Vaward Battle of about 500 men-at-arms when he met the leading column of the Swiss army. He kept his other two Battles mounted, believing his Vaward Battle capable of defeating the Swiss column, for the main body of the Swiss was not yet within supporting distance. The Swiss were indeed almost defeated but were relieved just in time by the main body, which threw the Austrians back. Leopold hurriedly dismounted his second Battle and led them to the attack but they were disordered and before they could arrive the Vaward Battle broke and the Swiss advanced on Leopold himself. The third Austrian line rode off at this vital moment and the Austrians with Leopold were surrounded and cut down, Leopold being slain by a halberd stroke.

The Swiss were equally successful against a feudal army at Näfels in 1388, but at Arbedo in 1422 they met the Italians for the first time and were severely handled. The Italians began the battle with a costly cavalry charge but, having learnt about the pike the hard way, followed it up with an attack by 6,000 dismounted men-at-arms in a single column against the Swiss phalanx of about 4,000, of whom two-thirds were armed with halberds, only one-third with cross-bows and pikes. The Swiss were on the verge of defeat when a new Swiss force appeared in the rear of the Italians, who drew off to counter this new threat. But the newcomers were only 600 foragers and made no attempt to advance further. The Swiss main body took advantage of the lull to retire from the field.

Mainly because of this experience the Swiss now adopted the pike as their main weapon and their reputation as the finest infantry in Europe was established in 1444 when at the battle of St Jacob-en-Birs less than a thousand Swiss pikemen attacked an army of Armagnac mercenaries outnumbering them by fifteen to one. The Swiss broke the Armagnac centre but were then surrounded by overwhelming numbers and forced to form hedgehog. For the remainder of the day they remained stationary in this formation, repelling charge after charge by heavy cavalry, interspersed with hails of missiles from the French light troops, and by the end of the day all the Swiss were dead; but they were surrounded by the corpses of 2,000 French. From that day forward, and until the sixteenth century, the Swiss remained superior to all other infantry and fully capable of withstanding the finest cavalry – and even defeating it.

Although the pike was now the main weapon of the Swiss, the halberd was retained to guard the banners, together with the two-handed sword men. If a column of pikes was halted by a stubborn foe these halberdiers would issue from the sides and rear of the column to attack the enemy's flanks and break the deadlock.

One of the great advantages the Swiss had over their enemies during their long fight for independence was their speed of assembly. In an emergency an army of 20,000 pikes could be mustered and put into the field within three days, and such an army was not divided by the petty jealousies of the feudal armies, each man knowing his place in a column and the men of a canton fighting together under their cantonal banner, just as the English bowmen fought alongside kinsmen and friends from the same parish. This had an important effect on morale and, coupled with the ability of the pike columns to advance very rapidly for over a mile with the front ranks of pikes levelled, enabled them to force an enemy to fight where and when they chose.

Their officers were elected by the cantons and the tactics for each battle were decided by a council of war of these officers. The usual order of battle was an advance in echelon of three columns, the leading column making for a fixed point in the enemy line while the central column marched parallel and slightly to the left or right rear. The third column was still further back and frequently halted when battle was joined in order to observe the result before becoming committed. Sufficient room was left between the columns for wounded, disarmed and defeated men to retreat and regroup at the rear of the columns. There were a number of variations of this basic battle order. Sometimes the centre column would lead and both flanks would be refused, or the two flanks advanced and the centre was refused. The columns varied in strength from about 2,000 men in the early days to 5–6,000 later on, but sometimes there would be very large right and centre columns and a small left, or on occasions an enormous right and a small centre and left.

The Swiss columns did not suffer the fate of the Flemish hedgehogs or Scottish schiltrons because they were always preceded and supported by light troops who formed from ten to twenty-five per cent of the army: Morat, where 10,000 out of 35,000 were light troops, is an exceptional example of this emphasis on the importance of light troops. At first these troops were armed with the crossbow, but as early as 1388 handguns were used and these gradually replaced the crossbow during the fifteenth century. The role of the light troops was to screen the advance of the columns, drawing the enemy's fire upon themselves, cancelling the fire of archers, handgunners and cannon, and to shake the main battle line. When the pike columns were set for the charge the skirmishers fell back to the rear, where they reloaded and awaited the outcome.

The Swiss pike columns were fast, manoeuvrable and

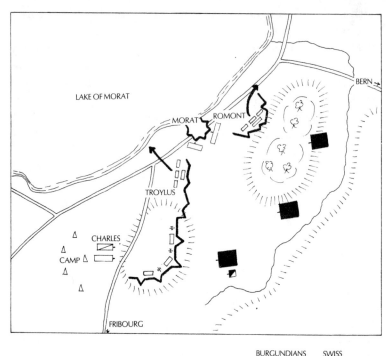

LAKE OF MORAT

MORAT · ROMONT

BERN →

TROYLUS

CHARLES

CAMP

FRIBOURG

BURGUNDIANS	SWISS	
◺	◼	CAVALRY
☐	■	INFANTRY

Morat, 1476. Charles of Burgundy had placed his Battles so that they could not support each other and failed to throw out a screen of light troops, although he knew the Swiss were nearby. This enabled the leading Swiss columns to march unobserved across his front to attack the weak forces behind the defences on his right. The disorganised troops advancing from the camp were overwhelmed piecemeal. The third Swiss column attacked the 6,000 men of Troylus and annihilated them and only the men from Savoy under Romont escaped the slaughter, marching across the rear of the Swiss.

struck with almost the shock of heavy cavalry, so that for most of the period with which we are concerned no other infantry and few cavalry could withstand their onslaught. At Arbedo it has been estimated that at least 400 horses were killed on the hedge of points in that first charge by the Italian cavalry. In the campaign of 1476–77 Charles the Bold

of Burgundy backed his feudal cavalry with English longbowmen, Flemish pikemen, German arquebusiers and
Italian men-at-arms, yet his army was defeated by the Swiss
pikes and Charles himself slain by the blow of a halberd
which split his skull in two. In 1498 600 pikemen from
Zurich were caught in the open by 1,000 Austrian cavalry
yet held off the Austrians easily by forming hedgehog.

After defeating the Burgundian army at Grandson,
Morat and Nancy during the 1476–77 campaign, the Swiss
began to hire themselves out as mercenaries and served in
most of the European wars of the late fifteenth century.
Only another column of pikes could stand up to their rapid

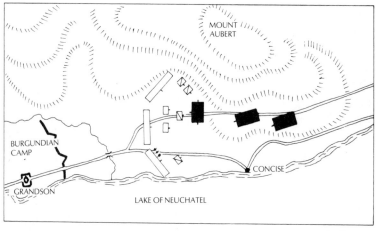

BURGUNDIANS : SWISS

◰   CAVALRY

☐ ■   INFANTRY

✦   GUNS

Grandson 1476. One of the three major battles of the Burgundian
campaign of 1476–77 against the Swiss. Here Charles the Bold attempted the classic double envelopment of Hannibal at Cannae, but the
infantry on his flanks, seeing the rapid advance of two more Swiss
columns and mistaking the withdrawal of the centre for a retreat, broke
and fled in panic. Prime cause of this panic was a lack of cohesion
between the various units of the Burgundian army; a common failing
in feudal armies.

advance and although many countries formed corps of pikemen none could withstand the Swiss until the arrival of the Landsknechts. These mercenaries were mostly Germans but they were not a national force like the Swiss and although they had good morale and were highly professional they were never quite up to the standard of the Swiss.

The only successful opponents of the pike during the fifteenth century were the Spanish, who mixed a strong force of sword-and-buckler men from Aragon with their pikemen. These swordsmen rose to a position of importance in warfare towards the end of the fifteenth century and were hired by many countries, but it was not until the battle of Barletta in 1502 that they met the *Swiss* pikemen. The Swiss pikes forced the Spaniards to open their ranks but under the cover of their bucklers the Spanish swordsmen got beneath the pikes and slaughtered the Swiss who, although armed with swords for close fighting, lacked the heavy armour and bucklers of the Spaniards. However, savage battles between the Swiss and the Landsknechts, and between the Swiss and the sword-and-buckler men, did not really get under way until the turn of the century, and consequently the tactics employed by them against each other fall outside the scope of this book.

The Condottieri

In Italy the predominance of hired companies of professional soldiers led to the evolution of a completely different system of warfare. Because the wars between the cities of Italy were mostly economic in motive, the captains of the mercenary companies tended to regard the wars as a business, and their men as their capital. Since most of the men fighting on both sides were hired professionals who might be on the same side next week, there was little point in fierce and bloody battles where friends might be killed, the captain's 'capital' severely diminished. Therefore the condottieri, who were mostly heavily armoured cavalry, avoided the mountains, marshes and water courses which were so inconvenient for cavalry and fought only on dry, open plains where the two sides could conduct a series of manoeuvres, perhaps culminating in a cavalry mêlée and a brief exchange of battering blows on each other's armour, until one side was deemed to have won the battle. (At the battle of Zagonara in 1423 three men died. At Molinella in 1427, which lasted half a day with neither side giving way, Machiavelli recorded that some horses were killed and men taken prisoner, but no man died. A later author, protesting at this slander, claimed that 300 men had been killed – out of 20,000 engaged!) Another method of waging war was to lay siege to an important city which the citizens did not want damaged or could not afford to lose, and attempt to obtain a surrender by encirclement. The besieged would conduct a number of raids to cut the supply lines of the condottieri and the first side to run out of food sued for peace. There was also a great deal of time spent in burning crops and destroying vineyards and orchards, for a successful war required money, which meant prosperous trade and agriculture: if you destroyed an enemy's crops you crippled his ability to maintain a mercenary army in the field. On the other hand, complete victory could end the employment of these armies, and so the wars tended to be dragged out for as long as the employer's patience and money would last.

This method of warfare received a rude shock when in 1439 many Venetians were killed by arquebusiers employed by Bologna. This was counted such an atrocity that when the Venetians won the battle they rounded up all the Bolognese who had carried arquebuses and executed them.

The Condottieri and their methods were crushed and swept aside when Charles VIII of France invaded Italy in 1494 with his national army.

The Hussite Wagenburg

Another system of tactics developed in the fifteenth century, which proved capable of defeating the feudal cavalry and levies of the Holy Roman Empire, was that devised by Jan Ziska, the commander of the puritan Hussite armies of Bohemia during the wars with Catholic Germany from 1419 to 1478.

The hopelessly outnumbered Czech nobility could not possibly employ the traditional cavalry-versus-cavalry tactics in these wars and therefore Ziska organised the peasants and burghers of the levy into a fighting force capable of standing up to the cavalry on its own. Ziska had seen the goliaigorod (moving fortress) used by the Russians when attacked on the march – the drawing into a circle of the wagons accompanying the army to form a barrier with-in which the cavalry could be protected. Obviously the Czechs' only chance lay in such defensive measures and in the first months of the war Ziska ordered entrenchments dug round all the towns to give him time to raise and train this new army. At first he used any carts and wagons which were available, but later he had specially reinforced wagons constructed which carried small cannon and were fitted with hooks and heavy chains to link them together. Within these moving fortresses his infantry were safe from the heavy cavalry of the Holy Roman Empire, and was quite capable of dealing with the feudal levies.

Soon he was able to develop the wagenburg into an offensive weapon by continual training, just as the Swiss had advanced the use of the pike. A special corps of wagoners was formed which could manoeuvre the wagons into a circle, square or triangle at a word of command, and speedily disengage the teams and chain the wagons together. Each wagon was allocated ten missile men and another ten pike and flail men guarded each gap between the wagons. From the very beginning Ziska made use of handguns – almost one third of the missile men had firearms, and the army was supported by a strong train of artillery which included bombards capable of throwing projectiles up to 100 pounds in weight.

The basic order for a Hussite army on the march was five

parallel columns; the cavalry and artillery in the centre, flanked on each side by two divisions of wagons with their infantry. The two inner wagon columns were shorter than the outer ones and at the word of command could be rapidly moved into position at the head and rear of the army to form a rectangular defence formation.

Ziska's wagenburg first defeated Sigismund's feudal host at Prague in 1420, to the surprise of the entire Holy Roman Empire, which responded by raising ever larger armies instead of abandoning the traditional tactics. The Hussites won again and again: at Deutschbrod in 1422 and, after Ziska's death, at Aussig in 1426 and Taus in 1431. Often the German levies could not be made to attack the wagenburg, against which the cavalry was useless and, gaining experience and morale, the Hussites took to advancing from their defences and defeating armies numerically their superior. Small bands of only a few thousand men laid waste to Bavaria, Meissen, Thuringia and Silesia without encountering any serious opposition.

The only real threat to the wagenburg tactics was gunfire at the wagons themselves, but the Hussite artillery was usually more than sufficient to silence the enemy guns and it was not the Holy Roman Empire but the Czechs themselves who first defeated the wagenburg when in 1434 the Czech moderates and the extremist Taborites met at the battle of Lipan. The moderates attacked the Taborite wagenburg, were repulsed and the Taborites, forgetting they were no longer fighting the levies of the Emperor, rushed out to pursue the fleeing enemy, who turned and fought back fiercely. A cavalry reserve swiftly rode between the Taborites and their wagons and the extremists were then cut to pieces on the open plain. The battle illustrates the basic weakness of the wagenburg – it was primarily a defensive weapon which was only successful against the out-dated tactics of the feudal nobility, and against steady troops under the command of an intelligent and experienced general it could be rendered ineffective. Henry VIII of

England had some armoured wagons for his handgunners in the new army of the sixteenth century, but otherwise the tactics were not generally employed elsewhere in Europe, although they were known. For example, in 1429 Sir John Fastolf, en route to the besiegers' lines at Orleans with a train of wagons containing provisions, was attacked by 8,000 French men-at-arms. He drew the wagons into a circle and easily repulsed the French attacks with his 2,000 archers and spearmen.

The Hungarians and the Handgun

During the fourteenth and fifteenth centuries the Turks overran the Balkan peninsula as far as the line of the Danube and the Save, and it was only the resistance of the Hungarians in the second half of the fifteenth century which enabled this line to be held. Until the middle of the century the feudal cavalry of Hungary was the equal of the feudal cavalry of the Turks, but about this date the Turks began to use larger numbers of infantry – the famous Janizaries, armed with the bow, later the crossbow. Suleiman the Magnificent, sultan from 1520 to 1566, had about 12,000 Janizaries. Since the Hungarians had no native infantry they began hiring European mercenaries, mainly pikemen and arquebusiers. In 1444 at the battle of Varna, the Hungarian chivalry attempted to break the Turkish line by a headlong charge in the traditional manner but was broken by the bows of the Janizaries. Therefore, four years later, at the battle of Kossovo, the Hungarian cavalry was supported by mercenary infantry, mostly handgunners from Germany: the first major confrontation between the crossbow and the handgun.

The Turkish line consisted of the Janizaries armed with crossbows in the centre, flanked by great masses of light cavalry armed with lance, bow, sword and mace. The Hungarians placed their handgunners opposite the Janizaries and their light cavalry, or hussars as they were already called, on the flanks. The Turks had 100,000 men; the Hungarians 24,000 Hungarians, Poles, Wallachians and the Germans. For two days the battle raged, the two centres exchanging bolts and bullets while the cavalry made successive charges against each other. At a critical moment during the second day's fighting the Wallachians treacherously deserted to the Turks and the Hungarian cavalry was defeated. However, the centre still held and the Hungarians were able to withdraw, leaving 8,000 of their nobility dead on the field.

The significant points of this battle were the introduction of professional infantry into a sphere previously dominated by the cavalry arm, and the fact that by mid-century the handgun was already effective enough to hold the centre against a large force of crossbowmen, and, supported by pikemen, continue to fight even when the supporting cavalry was defeated.

CHAPTER FIVE

Castles and other Fortifications

The Castle and its Role

THE castles which were garrisoned and fought over during the 1300–1500 period represented all stages in castle development from the stone motte and bailey castle of the eleventh century to the great concentric castles of the late thirteenth century and it' is therefore necessary to trace the entire evolution of stone castles. The designing and building of castles had reached its peak by the end of the thirteenth century and during the fourteenth and fifteenth centuries there were no major advances, merely improvements to or adaptations of existing designs. Some of these variations will be described later.

Castles were very much alike throughout Europe, and the only factor which caused preference to be given to one design or another was the terrain, for the primary concern was always that the design should make full use of advantageous features in the terrain.

It is important to remember that the castle was not a place of refuge, but a centre of military power from which the surrounding countryside could be dominated, or a vital pass commanded, or a seaport or trade route along a river be protected. Therefore, a castle's garrison frequently contained a large proportion of mounted men who patrolled an area with a radius of about thirty miles. In times of siege, sorties were often made from the postern gates, for even under siege conditions the castle maintained its ability to take aggressive action.

The castle was also a storehouse for munitions, an advanced headquarters and observation post in troubled areas, the home of a lord, and a place where he could be secure from attacks by his enemies. Royal castles could in times of emergency act as havens for the king's field army, or supply the men to raise a new army if the field army was defeated. In the advent of an invasion castles drew off large numbers of men from the invading force, which had to capture or at least contain the castles being left in the rear or on the flanks to maintain supply and communication lines.

Motte and Bailey Castles

The motte and bailey castle of the eleventh and twelfth centuries consisted of a large mound (the motte) topped by a wooden keep or tower and surrounded by a palisade and ditch, and an enclosure for accommodation, stables, livestock pens, etc. (the bailey), which was defended by another palisade and ditch. The palisade of the bailey often continued up the motte to connect with the palisade there. Entrance was via a bridge and through a gate flanked by wooden towers to the bailey, then through another gate and over a bridge spanning the inner ditch to the top of the motte. The entrance to the keep itself was on the first floor, access being by ladder only. This basic design proved strong enough to survive until the fourteenth century, but it had one major weakness: the defences formed a series of barriers which could not support each other and so allowed the besieger to concentrate his forces against each barrier in turn. Nevertheless, castles of motte and bailey design were built and inhabited throughout the medieval period.

The motte and bailey castle began to be reconstructed in stone during the twelfth century. The bailey palisade was replaced by a stone wall (the curtain wall), often plain but in some cases battlemented, with towers guarding the gate and sometimes towers set into the wall at intervals. The wooden tower on the motte was replaced by one of two distinct types of keep. The easiest and cheapest type was the shell keep, which was simply a stone wall following the line of the motte palisade, with the dwellings which replaced the tower built against this wall, leaving an open courtyard in the centre. Its main advantage was that it could be added quickly to the older fortifications, and its comparatively light weight enabled it to be built on newly erected artificial mottes which might subside under heavy keeps. However, it was inferior to the tower keep, which relied on passive defence in the form of high and thick walls, a combination which proved to be very effective.

Because of the great weight of stone employed in tower keeps most were built only on natural mounds, and where the motte was artificial, or unsuitable for the rectangular plan of a tower keep, the keep was built within the bailey. Therefore, most new castles with tower keeps did not have a motte. The tower keep continued to be used for as long as castles had a military role to fulfil.

The walls of tower keeps were on average 14 ft. thick and 50 ft. high, supported by pilasters along the walls and turrets at the corners, with the base splayed out to form a plinth to resist such siege weapons as the ram, bore and pick. An average keep would have a ground plan say 60 by 50 ft. At the lowest levels there were slits for ventilation and light; they were not designed as arrow slits at this stage. From the second floor up, the windows were about 2 ft. wide and 5 ft. long, but were few in number and were heavily barred and shuttered in times of unrest. The larger windows made in the walls from the thirteenth century on were protected by iron grilles. Entrance to the keep was usually on the first floor, occasionally on the second, and steps to the doorway

The twelfth century castle of Loches, south-east of Tours. The great tower keep is 130 ft. high, 80 ft. long and 45 ft. wide.

were built at right angles to this entrance, either against the keep wall or separate from it, when the gap was bridged by a small drawbridge. Doorway and drawbridge were often protected by a small forebuilding.

The interior of the tower keep followed a more or less general pattern, being divided by a strong cross wall so that should the entrance to the keep be forced the defenders could retire behind yet another line of defence. The cross wall was solid at ground level except for a small doorway, but on the residential floors was usually pierced by large arches to give more space and light.

Spiral staircases were built in one or more of the corners of the keep to connect the floors and were continued up to the corner turrets. The spiral was normally right-handed so that defenders retreating to the towers would have plenty of room to swing their swords while the central pillar of the stairs protected their left side. Conversely, the enemy had no room to swing his sword and his shield was practically useless. The stone surround of the well was usually extended up to the residential floors for convenience and greater security.

During the twelfth century it became obvious that the great weakness of the tower keep was its corners, which were comparatively easy to break up with siege weapons, and could not be protected except by men stationed directly overhead, who must expose their bodies to the enemy in order to fire at the attackers below. No other defensive fire could be brought to bear on the bottom of these exposed corners. The obvious answer was a round keep, which began to develop in the second half of the century. Orford Castle in Suffolk, built between 1165 and 1173 for Henry II, was one of the first of these new-style keeps and represents a transitional stage for, although perfectly cylindrical inside, the outer face was broken by three great buttresses which were again a weak point, though they could be defended more adequately than the corners of the tower keeps.

The first truly cylindrical keeps do not appear until the thirteenth century but, despite their advantage over the tower keep, they never became widespread. This was mainly because just as the design had been perfected the hitherto unchallenged belief that the keep was the ultimate stronghold of a castle was made obsolete by new developments in castle design.

Curtain Wall Defences

Until the thirteenth century the basic principle of the motte
and bailey castle had persisted; unco-ordinated lines of
defence in depth. The original plan had been improved
somewhat by adding a second bailey to create an inner and
an outer bailey, each with its own wall and gate to be over-
powered, but advances in the sphere of siege warfare had
now made it possible for the besiegers to breach the bailey
walls with comparative ease and even in some cases cause
the downfall of the mighty keep itself. Château Gaillard,
one of the finest castles in western Europe and considered
impregnable when built in 1197–1198, was captured only
five years after its completion. In 1215 and 1224 the great
English tower keeps of Rochester and Bedford were undermined. In each of these cases the castles were reduced
systematically, the besiegers concentrating their assault on
one line of defence at a time.

During the early thirteenth century new ideas on fortification began to spread through Europe from the East.
Many new features began to be added to existing castles or
incorporated into new ones, and the emphasis began to shift
from the keep to the bailey walls; obviously it was better
to keep an enemy out altogether than have the bailey – and
perhaps even the great keep – overrun and sacked. The
bailey walls already had battlements to provide cover for
archers and a wall walk, or allure, to allow movement
along the top of the wall. These measures allowed besiegers to be held off or repulsed from the top of the wall,
but there was no defence against an enemy using siege
weapons at the base of the wall except by leaning over the
battlements and thus becoming exposed to waiting marks-
men. The bases of walls and towers were battered for extra
strength but this was not a permanent solution to the
problem. The answer was to keep the enemy away from the
base of the walls, and this could only be achieved by greater
fire power. The merlons – the raised part of the battle-

The cylindrical keep of Gaillard Castle, built 1197–1198 by Richard I
to keep the French out of Normandy.

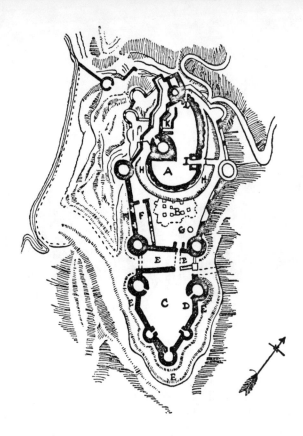

Plan of Gaillard Castle showing the incorporation of new ideas into the basic motte and bailey design, including the concentric principle in that the middle ward enclosed the inner ward, which enclosed the keep, each outer wall being lower in turn. A. inner ward, B. middle ward, C. outer ward, D. gate, E. ditches, F. chapel, G. well, H. inner moat, I. entrance to inner ward, L. postern gate.

ments· – were narrowed to permit a greater number of embrasures, and early in the thirteenth century the merlons themselves were pierced. The coping stones on top of the merlons were angled to deflect arrows upwards, and shutters were fitted to the embrasures, which gave archers more time to select a target and aim. Towards the end of the thirteenth century fire-power was increased still further by building one or two firing galleries into the walls below the rampart, thus doubling or trebling the number of arrow

The curtain wall of Pembroke Castle with pierced merlons and a second, lower, row of arrow slits.

slits in the walls.

Another method of protecting the base of the walls was the brattice or hoarding, a covered wooden platform built on the front of the battlements to allow missiles and stones to be discharged through slots in the floor. These had been in use since the twelfth century. Hoardings were normally of a temporary nature, being taken to pieces and stored in times of peace. They were vulnerable to missiles from siege engines and on the Continent they were replaced by stone machicolation by *c.* 1200 onwards, machicolation being the building outwards of a parapet on corbels so that missiles could be hurled through the created aperture. Machicolation did not become common in Britain until the end of the fourteenth century and even then was restricted mainly to gatehouses.

Perhaps the greatest advance was the flanking tower, which first began to appear in western Europe in the last quarter of the twelfth century. Before this date square towers had been set flush with the bailey wall, but the flanking tower projected outside the bailey wall, enabling the defenders to fire from slits in the sides of the towers along the outer face of the bailey wall. Such towers, correctly sited, provided covering fire for each other and divided the allure into sections so that a captured section could be isolated and dominated by the men in the towers. The towers were capped by steep, conical roofs which helped to deflect missiles thrown by siege engines. The earliest flanking towers were often three-sided with an open back. This was an advantage if they were captured, since there was then no shelter for the attackers, but a disadvantage in that the tower was not an individual stronghold. Later towers did not have this open back.

The advantages of cylindrical keeps over square or rectangular ones also apply to flanking towers, and by the mid-thirteenth century most new towers were round. The earliest examples of round or half-round towers occur at the end of the twelfth century.

Flanking towers in the east wall of Angers Castle on the Loire, built 1228–1238 on solid rock. Note the battering of the tower bases.

The early fourteenth century barbican of Lewes Castle in Sussex, which formerly had two portcullis and drawbridges in addition to the machicolation.

The Keep-Gatehouse

The next step came with the increasing use of mercenaries instead of vassals for garrison duty. During the eleventh and most of the twelfth centuries the gateway in the bailey wall had been protected by a square tower each side. Towards the end of the twelfth century this arrangement was strengthened by the use of four towers, two on each side of the opening linked by short walls, providing a defence in depth. By mid-thirteenth century rounded towers had replaced the square ones and in the late thirteenth century–early fourteenth century this idea was developed into the great gatehouse, the towers being joined together above the gateway to form a long narrow passage, blocked at each end by a portcullis and gates. The passage was further defended by the use of pits, arrow slits in the side walls, and 'murder holes' in the floor above, through which missiles or water could be hurled, a common method of defeating these defences being the use of fire in the passage to burn down the gates and roast the defenders above.

These great gatehouses were evolved because the use of mercenaries had led the castle owner to revise his position within the castle. Mercenaries were far different to feudal vassals and might easily mutiny; there was therefore no point being safe within a keep if you could not control the gateway into the castle. This factor led to the keep-gate-house, which allowed the lord to house his family safely in the gatehouse, where he could keep control of the entrance to the castle.

Unlike the keep, which was used for last stands, the keep-gatehouse was in the forefront of the fighting. Frequently it could only be entered from the ramparts at first floor level, having no doors on the ground floor, and this meant that even if the gates and the remainder of the castle fell the gatehouse could continue to resist in the same way as the tower keep.

Because the gatehouse was so strong, from the late

thirteenth century on many castles had two main gates and two or three postern gates. This greater freedom of movement enabled the defenders to sally out to take the offensive more easily, and therefore the gatehouse acted in support of the other defences by forcing the besieger to invest the whole perimeter of the castle, thus preventing him from concentrating all his forces at any one point.

Additional defences or outworks, called barbicans, were often built to protect the gatehouse, acting like small baileys. In their simplest form they consisted of two parallel walls built out at right angles to the gatehouse, thereby forcing an attacker to approach the gates by a narrow defended passage. Sometimes the outer end of the barbican might be covered by another work, such as a tower, or by its own complex of moat, drawbridge and gate.

Concentric Castles

The greatest period for castle building began in the last quarter of the thirteenth century with the arrival in western Europe of the concentric castle. These castles were similar to the ones developed in Syria by the Crusaders and consisted of a circuit of walls and towers, usually quadrangular in plan, surrounded by another lower wall with its own flanking towers. The area between these two walls, usually very narrow, was divided by cross walls so that any force penetrating the outer wall could be confined to one sector, which would then act as a killing ground. The higher inner wall provided a covering fire for the outer wall. Perhaps the finest concentric castle in Britain, certainly the largest, with an area of thirty acres, is Caerphilly Castle in South Wales. Added to the basic strength of the concentric castle is an extensive system of water defences, barbican and outworks. The magnitude and strength of such defences is best illustrated by the accompanying plan.

It should be borne in mind that not all building of the thirteenth century was of new castles, and that by far the

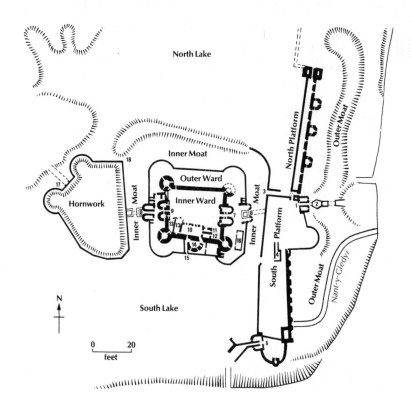

North Lake

North Platform

Outer Moat

Inner Moat

Outer Ward

18

17

Hornwork

Inner Ward

Inner Moat

Inner Moat

South Platform

Outer Moat

Nant-y-Gledyr

N

South Lake

0   20
feet

KEY

Eastern Front, comprising North and South Platforms

1. Main Gateway
2. Barbican and double drawbridge
3. Channel from Inner to Outer Moat
4. Watermill
5. South Gateway

Inner and Outer Wards

6. East Gate to Outer Ward
7. East Gate to Inner Ward
8. West Gate to Outer Ward

9. West Gate to Inner Ward
10. Great Hall
11. Buttery, etc.
12. Chapel
13. State Rooms
14. Kitchen Tower
15. Water Gate and covered passage
16. Storehouse

Hornwork

17. Gateway and site of drawbridge
18. Gateway and site of drawbridge

Caerphilly Castle, South Wales, built late thirteenth century.

greater bulk during this century took the form of adaptation and strengthening of existing defences. The Tower of London, for example, was extensively modernised in the thirteenth century and developed into one of the largest concentric castles in Britain, making obsolete the massive tower keep of the Normans.

Where conversion to the concentric plan was not possible because of the lie of the land, the new ideas were still utilised. For example, at Chepstow Castle in Monmouthshire a new bailey was added to each end of the original castle, both defended by drum towers and massive gatehouses. At many other castles development took place piecemeal, with the addition of gatehouses and flanking towers at the weakest spots on the walls, with the result that many castles retained their basic motte and bailey plan. Others, in less strategic positions, or owned by less wealthy lords, remained as built in the preceding centuries.

Fourteenth Century Castles

Although there were no new developments in castle design during the fourteenth century some new castles were built in the second half of the century which broke away from previous designs. The Hundred Years War placed a continual drain on manpower, yet produced professional soldiers, and these two factors had the effect of causing new castles to be smaller and simpler, requiring only small, permanent garrisons of professionals. Queenborough, built in 1361 on the Isle of Sheppey, is the finest example of such a castle in Britain. Employing the circular plan throughout, it had only one main gateway, on the west side, with access to the inner ring of defences on the east side, so that any attacker gaining entry through the outer gate had to make a half circuit of the bailey to reach the inner entrance, all the time under intense fire. On the east side of the outer wall was a postern gate to allow sallies by the garrison. Another vital point was the use of cross walls to divide the

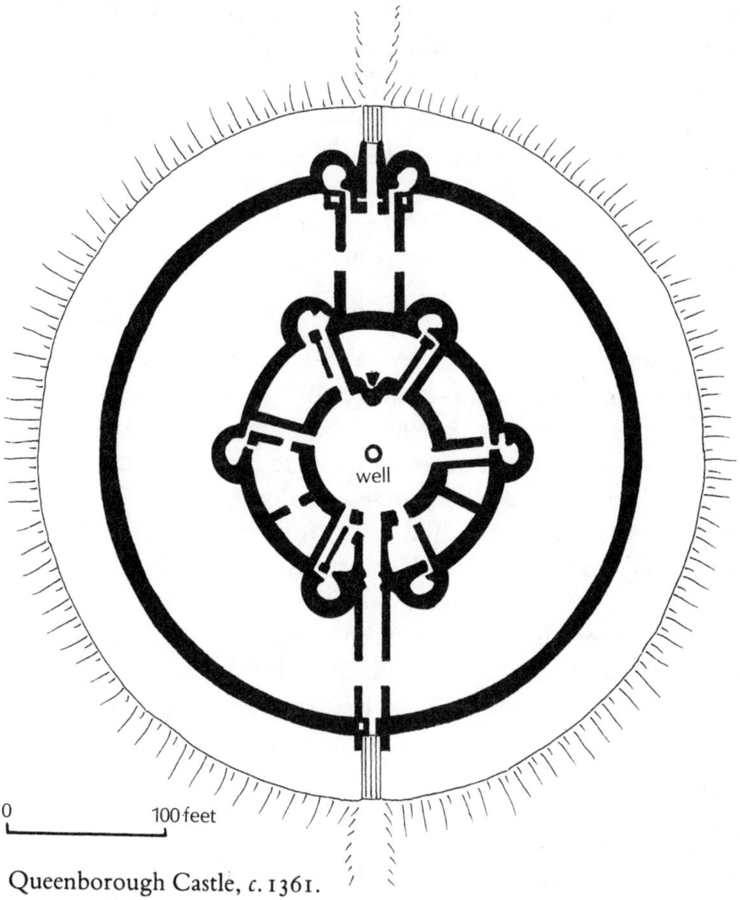

Queenborough Castle, *c.* 1361.

outer bailey into two and also funnel the attacker up a narrow passageway before being able to turn away, all the time subjected to fire from two towers and the wall. The other notable point is that the centre of the castle was kept clear to allow the small garrison to move quickly from point to point.

By the late fourteenth century castles were so strongly built that the only way to bring about their downfall – until the arrival of large and effective siege guns in the second half of the fifteenth century – was a long and costly siege to starve the garrison into submission. Consequently the castle as a focal point in war was avoided and battles were as much as possible fought well away from the sphere of influence of castles. Therefore, shutting oneself up in a castle no longer solved anything and from this date the importance of the castle began to decline, the castle eventually being replaced by the fortified manor house.

Fortified Manor Houses

The castle had always been a fortress *and* a home. The decline of the military role inevitably led to residential considerations becoming predominant and the new 'castles' built during the fifteenth century were mostly no more than fortified manor houses. These buildings were not a new development, for they had been built by the lesser gentry who could not afford castles since the end of the thirteenth century. Typical features of such buildings are large windows, numerous entrances at ground level, the thinness of the walls, and the use of brick instead of stone.

Moated Homesteads

Moated homesteads, or farms, appear during the fourteenth century, built by lesser gentry or small landowners who lived in open country, away from the safety of the towns, yet lacked the means to build a fortified manor house. A typical homestead would be rectangular in plan with the main dwelling forming one side, barns and sheds the other three, all surrounding an open courtyard in which livestock could be secured for the night. All windows opened on to this yard, as did most doors, thus presenting an outer face pierced by only one, perhaps two stout doorways. The whole was surrounded by a wet moat from 30 to 80 ft. wide and with an average depth of 10 feet. Towards the end of the fifteenth century some homesteads had windows in the outer walls.

European Castles

Until now we have discussed castle design in general terms for the whole of Europe, but regional differences did sometimes affect the construction, number and placing of castles in different countries. For example, Russia, Poland and Hungary were well timbered but had little stone and during the fourteenth century Tartar invasions, their wooden fortifications were burnt and the countries overrun. It was a different story when the Tartars came to the mountain regions of Czechoslovakia and Yugoslavia, where they were confronted by inaccessible stone castles commanding the vital passes.

The main differences occur chiefly in central Europe and the Iberian peninsula. During the twelfth and thirteenth centuries central Europe was ravaged by internal struggles and near-anarchy prevailed. Because of this many cities made their own provisions for defence, extending their defences along their trade routes in the form of numerous watch-towers and small castles. Because of the mountainous nature of the region, particularly southern Germany, Switzerland and Austria, there was a predominance of mountain fortresses which were of necessity small. Therefore, in this part of Europe castles were numerous but small and simple in design, unlike the French and British castles which tended to be large, complex and fewer in number.

Many of the castles of central Europe could not follow the recognised patterns described previously because of their site. One popular technique was to build a wall round the summit of a peak, then construct all the buildings within this perimeter – rather like a shell keep. Because of the difficulties in delivering materials and working on the site such castles were expensive and small, but the resulting eyrie provided great security. Another popular technique was to build on a spit of land jutting out into a river or lake, then isolate the castle with a wide moat. Tower keeps remained popular even in the fourteenth century but the

Stahleck Castle, Bacharach-on-the-Rhine.

interiors were different to those of French and English
castles, tending to have a series of moderate-sized rooms
instead of a great hall with small rooms grouped round it.

In Spain the major difference occurred in the interiors, for
the Spanish castle was not the home of a lord but the
barracks of a garrison to hold land regained from the
Moors. The tower keep remained popular for much longer
than elsewhere and the concentric design did not appear in
Spain until many years after its introduction into other parts
of Europe. Portugal followed the Spanish trends for the
same reasons, and most of the castles built before the thirteenth century are of the motte and bailey type. One of the
most interesting Iberian castles is that of Amieira, a concentric castle built in the second half of the fourteenth
century. The Moorish influence shows particularly in the
main gateway, which passes under one of four large, square
towers placed one at each corner of a central court.

Scandinavian castles follow basically the same styles and
development as the rest of north and west Europe. Kalmar
Castle, regarded as the key to Sweden, is virtually a concentric castle.

Walled Towns and Cities

In England the Normans had established their kings with
the aid of castles and by the second half of the thirteenth
century the country was fairly quiet, but in the rest of
Europe, particularly in Italy, conditions were far less settled.
In Europe strife was mainly caused by commercial rather
than political ambition so, although many castles were built,
there also developed a much greater number of fortified
towns and cities than are found in England.

In Italy the most notable were Genoa, Pisa, Florence and
Bologna, the last two each having over a hundred towers on
their walls. In Spain the greatest of all surviving Spanish
fortifications is the city of Avila, built between 1090 and
1099, with two miles of granite walls, eighty-eight towers

Kalmar Castle on the Baltic.

and nine main gates, each defended by flanking towers. An outstanding medieval town in France, and one which has survived to this day, is Carcassonne, guarding the road to Spain. The Roman fortifications here were extensively repaired in the second half of the thirteenth century and strengthened by the addition of towers and a moat. Avignon also retains much of its circuit of walls, towers and gates.

The walls of Avila, north-west of Madrid; a perfect example of the walled towns found all over medieval Europe.

The walls of Carcassonne, south-east of Toulouse. Although much restored in the nineteenth century by Viollet-le-Duc the town is a good example of medieval fortifications.

In England stone walls began to replace the earthen ramparts of the Saxons during the first half of the thirteenth century due to the Baronial Wars and the threat of invasion from France. At first the new fortifications were restricted to those towns which had old Saxon or Roman defences, such as Chester, Colchester and Exeter, but later a tax was instituted to allow more towns to be fortified, nearly fifty per cent of this tax being spent on the fortification of towns in Wales. Town defences declined in the first half of the fourteenth century, except along the Scottish border and the south east coast, but the advent of the Hundred Years War stimulated more fortification in the south because of fear of a French invasion, as indeed it did in France itself; Paris was rewalled in the middle of this century. The Wars of the Roses in the second half of the fifteenth century also provoked a spate of fortification so that by the end of this century there were few towns of any importance which did not have walls.

By the middle of the thirteenth century stone walls were a common defence for towns and cities throughout Europe. In the majority of these defences the walls were used primarily as a passive barrier linking together the towers. Offensive action could only be taken from the battlements and, as we have seen, this was not sufficient to protect the base of the wall. Hoardings are known to have been used at some of the larger and more vulnerable towns in 'frontier' areas and some town walls did have a second row of arrow slits at ground level, the allure then being supported by arches spanning the ground level slits.

As with castles, flanking towers were used to command the base of the walls but were rarely used effectively to break the circuit of the allure or in their role as individual strongholds, most town defences being designed and built by local masons who had no real knowledge of the art of fortification. (This does not apply, of course, to such great cities as Florence, Paris and London, or important ports such as Calais, Genoa and the like, which employed military

The walls of Tenby, South Wales, built in the thirteenth century and strengthened in the fifteenth.

engineers of high reputation and skill.) The shape of the towers varied from a flat D-shape in the mid-thirteenth century to a round tower at the end of the century, the latter giving greater firepower along the walls but presenting a narrower front to the enemy. Square towers became predominant from the end of the fourteenth century. It is difficult to understand why this should have happened when the reverse occurred in castle building, but it may have been because cannon were now being mounted in some towers and others were being leased as accommoda-

The west gate of Canterbury town walls, built 1380.

tion, both of which usages would require a more roomy building.

The gate was the most important part of a town's defences and was often provided with all the finer assets of the castle gatehouse; machicolation, murder holes, portcullis, barbican and drawbridge. The earliest gates consisted of just the gate itself flanked by two square guard chambers, but at the end of the thirteenth century half-round towers were added to the face and by the middle of the fourteenth century this had developed into two large round towers flanking a narrow gateway. Later in the century four towers were used, linked by short stretches of wall, as for castle gatehouses, and this style became predominant during the second half of the century. A return to the less effective square shape occurred in the early fifteenth century, by which time gatehouses were also being used for accommodation.

After the 1360s newly built towers sometimes had gunports as well as arrow slits, but cannon were not used to any great degree in town defences because of their slow rate of fire, limited range and line of fire, and the vibration they caused in such a confined space. When Orleans was besieged by the English in 1428–29, seventy one cannon were employed on the city walls, but their effect seems to have been moral rather than material.

The walls of the lesser towns were not designed to withstand a great siege in the same manner as castles, and most of the non-strategic towns were incapable of withstanding the attacks of a determined army for more than a few days, partly because their defences were inferior to those of castles, and partly because a wall encompassing a town was too long to be adequately manned unless a large garrison had been placed inside. The defences were primarily designed to keep out beggars, lepers, thieves and the plague, to provide a safe market for trading, and to discourage marauding bands of unemployed mercenaries, but if strengthened and properly manned many were capable of a prolonged resistance.

In the case of larger towns and cities, those used as military depots or strategic links by an army, and the strategic ports, the defences were often as well constructed as those of the great castles and they were manned in times of war by large garrisons. Under these circumstances many of the larger towns and cities became as formidable as castles, and cities such as Calais, Rouen, Orleans and Florence withstood sieges lasting from six months to almost a year.

CHAPTER SIX

Siege Warfare

THE business of laying siege to a castle was a highly complex and costly affair and was not undertaken lightly. Frequently such sieges involved so many men and so much *materiel* that no other action could be undertaken by the army involved and once committed to such a siege there arose the problems of guarding against an attack by a relieving force, maintaining adequate supplies of food and forage, and epidemic diseases caused by the concentration of a large body of men in a small area for a long time. Therefore the first action taken by a potential besieger was to 'summon the castle', i.e. parley with the commander of the garrison and offer terms for a surrender, it not being dishonourable to yield a castle to superior forces if there was no hope of a successful defence or of the arrival of a relief force. The castle commander had three alternatives: surrender, fight, or compromise by agreeing to surrender if no help came within a time limit acceptable to both sides. Only when the commander had refused to surrender or come to terms did the grim business of a siege begin.

The first task facing the besieger was the establishment of

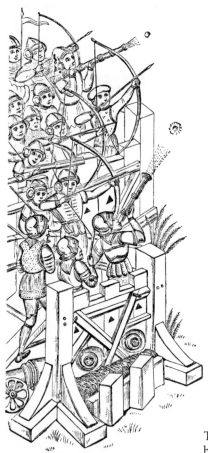

Timber fort erected before the
barbican of a castle, c. 1460–1480.

a camp, preferably near fresh water. The camp would have
to be protected against possible sallies by the garrison or
attack by a relief force and so a rampart or palisade, or both,
would be erected round the camp. A ditch would be dug,
the earth thrown up to form the rampart, and timber stakes
or wicker panels erected along the outer edge to provide
cover for the defenders. Sometimes such a palisade might
be within bowshot of the castle so that the garrison could be
kept under constant 'sniping' by archers and crossbowmen
enjoying the same degree of cover as the defenders. This had

the effect of providing a constant threat to one or even two sides of the castle, tying up a large percentage of the garrison. Sometimes, particularly by the second half of the fifteenth century, a timber fort might be erected from which crossbows, long or short bows, hand guns and cannon could all be discharged at the castle. Frequently this would be built opposite the main gate to prevent egress as well as to 'soften up' these defences, and from illustrations in the contemporary manuscripts such forts would appear to have been built of extremely heavy timbers. The defenders countered these measures by erecting forebuildings of a similar design in front of the gates and weak spots.

Barricades would be built across all roads to the castle in order to isolate it; timber would be gathered for the camp, forts and siege engines; stones collected and rounded for ammunition; and food and forage accumulated. (For the siege of Bedford Castle in 1224 by the king of England, some siege engines were built on the spot, others came from Lincoln and Northampton. Hides and timber also came from Northampton; ropes and cables for the engines from London, Cambridge and Southampton; and tallow, tents and pavilions for the king also from London. An army of carpenters, quarriers, masons and labourers was gathered from Lincoln, Bedfordshire and Northamptonshire, miners from Hereford and the Forest of Dean. Fifteen thousand crossbow bolts were ordered from Corfe Castle in Dorset, another 4,000 from Northampton.)

While this mass of material was being gathered and organised the commander of the besieging army would make a careful reconnaissance of the castle, accompanied by an experienced military engineer, analysing its defences and searching for the weak spots against which engines or assaults might be thrown with a decent chance of success. A few probing attacks might be made to sound out the defences in likely spots. After a council of war with the nobles, a plan of campaign would be mapped out, the necessary ladders, bridging materials, engines and so on constructed.

All this time small raids would be made against the castle to keep the defenders alert and attempt to deceive them as to the time and place of the main attack.

All this took considerable time and a relief force might well arrive before the preparations could be completed. In this case the siege might be called off, or the relief force defeated. In the latter case another truce might be held, offering the garrison a last chance to surrender, and if this were refused the costly assaults would begin, perhaps with the proviso that because of their refusal to surrender no quarter would be given to any occupants of the castle.

The commander of the besieging army had a choice of four methods of attack, not including intrigue and treason: over the walls by assault; through the walls via a breach created by bombardment or other means; under the walls by mining – in effect another method of creating a breach; and total blockade to reduce the garrison by starvation. Of these methods breaching the walls by bombardment was probably the best choice, for in this method it was possible to stay out of range of all enemy weapons except his artillery and methodically reduce the defences at one or two points until an assault could be made at small cost in lives. From the defender's point of view, prolonged bombardment was probably the greatest threat, for the only sure defence lay in a sally to destroy the engines, or at least some of them, for there might be several 'batteries'. This meant abandoning all the advantages of a defensive position. The only alternatives were to lower mattresses over the part being pounded in order to lessen the effect of the missiles, or repair fallen parts with timber or barrels filled with earth.

Siege Engines

There were three main types of siege engine, or 'gyns', each with its own distinctive method of propulsion, although these three types are referred to by a variety of names. The smallest type was the espringale, known in Roman times as the ballista, which was the father of the crossbow and resembled this weapon in construction except that it was on a larger scale. The espringale worked on the principle of tension and fired iron shafts or javelins about four ft long, though it could be adapted to fire stones. The Romans used the ballista in batteries as a field gun and the espringale was also used as an anti-personnel weapon, not for attacking the fortifications themselves. Effective range was about 150 yd with a flat trajectory which made them more accurate than the other engines. Both the attacker and defender used these weapons, the latter in particular to disrupt the firing of the larger engines, the former to pick off any man exposing himself on the battlements and therefore for counter-battery fire against the castle's espringales.

The second type of engine worked on the torsion principle and was called the mangonel or catapult. This could throw stones weighing up to 300 lb. to ranges of up to 400 yd with a slight trajectory, the object being to batter the defences down by repeated blows on the same spot. The stone was loaded into the spoon-shaped end of a wooden arm, the other end of which was thrust into a web of ropes secured to the frame. Horsehair or human hair was preferred for these ropes because it is more tensile. To load the weapon these ropes were twisted by means of capstans at the sides of the frame, the arm was then winched down to add a final twist and the stone placed in the spoon. When released, by a slip rope or hook and eye system discharged by a yank on a lanyard, the arm whipped up to strike a padded cross bar, catapulting the projectile in the same fashion as a paper wad being flicked from the end of a ruler which is allowed to strike the edge of a table.

The mangonel remained in use throughout the Middle Ages but from the end of the twelfth century was relegated to a secondary role by the arrival of a more powerful and accurate stone-throwing machine commonly known as the trebuchet. Gilles Colonne, who died in 1316, names four types of trebuchet, which he called a perrier, but all worked

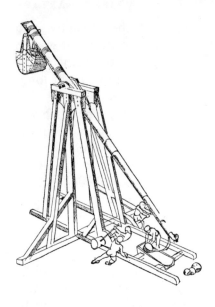

Trebuchet.

on the principle of counterpoise and consisted basically of a frame with a cross bar on which was pivoted a long arm, a quarter of which projected towards the enemy. To this short end was attached a container filled with weights, while the other end bore a sling. The sling end was winched down, a missile placed in the sling, and the arm suddenly released. The range could be altered by moving, or adjusting, the weight of the counterpoise on the short extension. Colonne refers to one type, where the counterpoise was movable, as the biffa; and another, which had one movable weight and another fixed to the beam, as the tripantum. The latter was supposed to have a greater range and accuracy than the trebuchet. The fourth type had a number of ropes in lieu of weights and these were pulled down by a group of men. This must have been a much smaller weapon, casting small stones, but having the advantage of being more rapidly loaded. It may have been a purely anti-personnel weapon.

Both mangonel and trebuchet were sometimes used to hurl the putrid corpses of horses over the walls in the hopes of spreading disease, or Greek fire (see pages 176–7) to set light to the inflammable parts of a fortress. Greek fire was also used as tracer on missiles hurled at night. The men who manned the siege engines, known as 'gynours', were a prime target for the archers of the castle, so no doubt night firing was used both to maintain a continuous bombardment and for the protection it afforded the crews.

Cannon

For most of the fourteenth century cannon were too small to play an effective part in siege warfare, although they were certainly used for sieges during this century. The cannon could fire only small balls at a slow rate, perhaps four an hour – the same rate as a trebuchet, and had the added disadvantage of often being as dangerous to the firer as to the target. Their use within fortifications was also limited because of the lack of room for recoil, and the damage the explosions caused to the stonework. In the last quarter of the century larger guns were available and in 1377 a cannon firing a 200-lb. ball was used at the siege of Ardres, but they were still unreliable, expensive, and most difficult to transport to the site of a siege, and therefore cannon continued to be subsidiary to the older engines for the whole of the fourteenth century and the early part of the fifteenth, the successful use of cannon against Harfleur in 1415 being the exception rather than the rule.

During the fifteenth century larger cannon became available which temporarily overtook the development of the fortifications opposing them, making them a vital piece of equipment for any besieging army. In 1424 English artillery battered down the walls of Le Mans within a few days, and during the great campaign of reconquest in 1449 the French took sixty fortresses with the aid of cannon, many surrendering as soon as they saw the big guns in position. (At Harcourt the first shot pierced the wall of the outer ward, which had been considered as strong as the wall of the keep itself.) The French were somewhat ahead of the

English, but the monstrous Mons Meg, still to be seen at Edinburgh Castle, and which fired a ball with a diameter of $19\frac{1}{2}$ in. and weighed 549 lb., dates from *c*.1460. Four years later the Earl of Warwick used two great cannon to reduce Bamburgh Castle, until that time considered impregnable. Even so, transportation of these pieces was still difficult, accidents continued to happen when firing them (James II of Scotland was killed in 1460 during a siege when a bombard blew up near him) and the mangonel and especially the trebuchet remained very much in evidence at sieges throughout the fifteenth century.

The largest cannon were laid on the ground for firing, usually held in position by a wooden framework, the crew protected by wattle or solid wood barriers with a shutter which was raised by ropes to allow the gun to be fired. Medium pieces were mounted on wooden or metal beds and often had frameworks which allowed them to be traversed and elevated – by driving wedges and chocks under the breech end for the large guns, by fitting the breech end into a quadrant for the smaller ones.

Mining

Whilst engines and cannon were pounding at the walls to effect a breach, mining operations might also be getting under way if the ground was suitable; many castles, especially the keeps, were built on solid rock, or were surrounded by a wet moat to prevent mining. Mining would begin some distance from the part of the walls to be attacked, the entrance being carefully concealed and the soil removed and hidden under cover of darkness, for the success of a mine depended on surprise. Having reached the part of the walls to be undermined, the soil would be excavated and the masonry propped up with timber. When a considerable cavern had been created under the defences the timbers supporting them were set alight by means of wood soaked in fat or petroleum, the miners withdrawing to watch from a discreet distance. The burning of the props usually resulted in the wall tumbling into the cavern, an assault often being timed to take advantage of the confusion as the wall fell. In the fifteenth century gunpowder was sometimes used to blow up the defences and in this case one or two right-angled bends were made in the shaft near its head to contain the explosion within the required area.

Mining was slow but sure, for there was no defence against a mine unless it could be detected in time. Members of a garrison were often detailed to listen for mining operations, and one method of discovering miners was to place bowls of water at suspected spots, the water revealing the slightest vibrations. If a mine was discovered in time a countermine could be dug and the enemy miners driven out by flood, smoke, or force of arms. These underground conflicts could be very savage and confused, but even the noblest of knights took part in them.

Breaching Weapons

If a castle could not be undermined, and if the artillery failed to make a breach, then a commander could still bring into action another selection of weapons to enable him to create a breach in the defences. These weapons were known by a variety of names, but all operated against the castle walls at close range and therefore needed a protective covering and access across the moat. Shelter was provided by a stout, rectangular framework mounted on thick wooden wheels and covered by a sloping timber roof, propelled by men inside it. The four sides were usually open, the roof frequently covered with green hides to resist fire. This shelter was known variously as a tortoise (either because of its speed or after the Roman shield formation), penthouse, rat, sow, or cat, the last no doubt from its slow and stealthy approach. The moat would be bridged for the passage of the cat by beams or filled in at that spot with earth, stones and timber, all of which could be positioned from the shelter of the cat itself. The cat was then pushed into position against the castle wall, its wheels wedged and one of a number of breaking up methods employed against the stonework.

Meanwhile the defenders would try to put the cat out of action by dropping large rocks on its roof, pouring boiling water or oil upon it and attempting to set fire to it. The slope and strength of the roof usually took care of the rocks, the hides sometimes resisted fire – but not always Greek fire, and the roof was normally made liquid-proof. The defenders attempted to overcome the latter precaution by driving long stakes into the roof to create cracks through which the boiling liquid could find an entrance.

Under cover of the cat miners might break down the wall with hand picks but more frequently other methods were employed. One of these was the ram or bosson, a huge baulk of timber suspended from the roof of the cat by chains and propelled against the wall by a team of up to sixty men. Some of these rams had a blunt metal head which ultimately broke up the masonry; others were less weighty and had a sharp metal point which pierced the masonry. These were called picks, bores or the mouse, the last from the appearance of gnawing away at the base of the wall, and required fewer men to work them. There were one or two smaller weapons with the same purpose which had a drill head and were revolved either by handles set at right angles to the beam or by a large bow on the same principle as the hand-operated bow drill.

We have already seen how the garrison attempted to destroy the cat; they also had a variety of methods for countering the action of the rams and picks. Large mattresses or a series of beams were lowered over the attacked part of the wall on chains to absorb the impact of the ram. Grapnels or large pincers were lowered on chains to engage the head of ram or pick and haul it up to such an angle that it became useless. A huge beam might be dangled horizontally to the ground from two long poles, operated from behind the cover of the walls and pivoted over the parapet, the poles

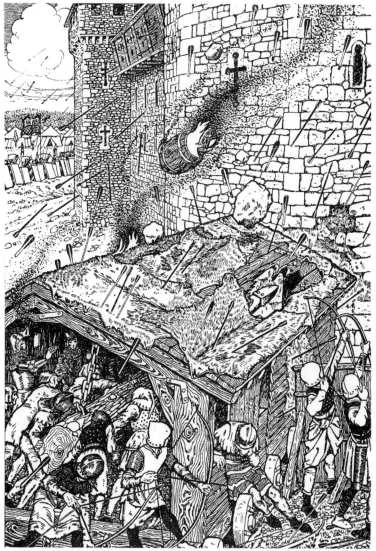

A cat equipped with a ram. Note the hoardings on the castle walls.

being used to raise and lower the beam, which might smash the roof of the cat or by a lucky blow break off the ram or pick head. If all these methods failed it would only be a short time before a breach was effected but even so all was not lost, for a barrier could be constructed to bridge the section of wall threatened. The barrier usually consisted of two rows of stakes lined on the inside with planks and the central part packed tightly with earth and stones. Often a scaffold was erected on the inner face to maintain contact along the top of the walls, and from this scaffold the defenders could begin their resistance all over again when the masonry was breached. Alternatively, if time did not permit the building of a barrier, the breach might be blocked by a ribauldequin, or a breach-piece consisting of a trestle framework bearing long spears interspersed with hand guns. This acted like a combination of *chevaux de frise* and ribauldequin and was very effective in slowing down an assault on a breach.

Covering Fire

While all these weapons were being brought forward and put to work both besiegers and defenders were constantly firing arrows and bolts at each other in an attempt to prevent the weapons and counter-measures being effective. The besieging archers and crossbowmen would have been at a considerable disadvantage on open ground and therefore pavises were usually employed, crossbowmen often slinging these on their backs and keeping their backs to the castle whilst loading, turning only to fire. A more effective defence was the mantlet, sometimes of wattle, sometimes planks or poles joined by cross-members. This was either carried forward and held up by a prop when firing, or fitted with a rear leg and three wheels to form a small mobile 'fort'. Arrows could be discharged round the edges of these shields, but often there was a slit in the mantlet which gave a more complete defence. Men behind such defences were the equivalent of the modern sniper and little could be done to prevent them picking off any defender who exposed himself. The humble slinger should not be forgotten here, for often a great part of the 'small arms' fire during a siege came

A belfry in action.

from the sling. The main advantage, apart from their known high degree of accuracy, was that ammunition was plentiful and volleys could be delivered in such rapid succession that defenders often found it impossible to reply.

Escalade

If all these methods of attack on the walls failed there remained only the most costly method of all – escalade. Scaling ladders might be used, the men on them holding their shields in such a way as to form a covered way, but these could be pushed away with forked poles before the first man could reach the top. Speed was the essential factor in such an attack, together with simultaneous assaults at several points in the defences and massive covering fire by the archers and crossbowmen. Where the walls were not too high scaling ladders with hooks at the top might be used, and often it was possible for a man to reach the top before the defenders could dislodge the hooks.

Ladder parties would not bother with filling in the moat at every point but would use planks or movable bridges to cross the ditch. The bridges were just a wooden platform on wheels, propelled by a long pole from the rear. The wheels were positioned near the rear edge of the bridge and removed, or allowed to slip over the edge of the ditch, once the bridge had spanned the moat.

A method more likely to succeed was the belfry or siege tower, a two- or three-storey wooden building covered with green hides as an anti-fire precaution. This had to be constructed well clear of the enemy's missiles and because it was heavy and clumsy a level path was prepared for it right up to the castle walls by men working under the cover of cats. For the same reasons such towers might often be little more than a covered 'cabin' on stilts, with ladders at the rear, but contemporary illustrations usually show them planked at front and sides. If the belfry was higher than the walls the top was battlemented and from this vantage point

A more primitive siege tower. Note the engine on the gatehouse and
the unusual wheeled shelter for cannon before the barbican gate.

archers would maintain a steady fire at the defenders while a
drawbridge was lowered on to the battlements of the castle.
The idea of the belfry was that the attackers should be on at
least equal terms with the defenders at the top of the wall,

Fifteenth century 'organ' gun, bombard and mortar at work during a siege.

and its main advantage was that once the drawbridge was in position a mass of men could be thrown against the defenders, who must be fewer in number at the assault point because of the narrow allure. Sometimes a ram would be installed in the lowest storey so that if the assault over the drawbridge failed another attempt could be made at breaching the walls. The main disadvantage of the tower was its clumsy, slow advance, during which the men propelling it were subjected to intense fire – as was the tower itself by the defenders' engines, which frequently used incendiaries in an attempt to set it alight.

Other Weapons

Mention has been made several times in this chapter of Greek fire. It is believed Greek fire consisted mainly of petroleum and oil, for it burnt on water, and that various additions were made for special purposes: pitch to make it burn longer, sulphur to make it stick, and quicklime to make it ignite on contact with water. These ingredients made it difficult to extinguish and many a cat and belfry must have come to grief because of it. Water had no effect upon it at all, smothering was often ineffective, and only sand, vinegar or urine – if available in sufficient quantities, could put it out. However, its main use was for incendiary arrows, which played an important part in siege warfare on both sides of the walls. Quicklime was also used on windy days to blind the enemy, having an effect rather like poisonous gas, and red-hot sand was sometimes used instead of boiling oil or water, all three being very effective at penetrating the chinks in armour. 'Stink pots' of burning sulphur were also used to bombard personnel.

One other weapon occasionally used to blow open gates or make holes in walls was the petard, an early limpet mine. It consisted of an iron pot filled with gunpowder and fixed to a board which prevented the powder coming out in transit. One or two hooks were attached to the edges of this board, allowing it to be fixed quickly against a wall or gate by hanging it from heavy nails driven into the target. A slow fuse at the closed end of the pot was lit once the mine was fixed. The largest petard held about fifteen lb. of gunpowder.

Blockade

Should every weapon and trick fail the besieger was left with no alternative but to establish a complete blockade around the castle – provided he was strong enough to hold off or defeat all relief forces – and wait until the castle's garrison was forced to submit or starve to death. This was certainly the easiest method of all, but it meant tying up a large army in the siege and was extremely expensive in manpower, materials and provisions. It was also the surest method of victory for, no matter how well stocked the

(A)

(B)

(C)

(D)

(E)

(F)

(G)

Scenes of siege warfare: a) primitive trebuchet; b) arming a knight;
c) siege tower; d) trench digging; e) crossbowman; f) stringing a longbow; g) trebuchet apparently about to launch a donkey into the defences.

(A)

(B)

(C)

(D)

(E)

Siege scenes from medieval manuscripts: a) covering fire from the battlements, hoardings and a mantlet; b) slaughtering horses and boiling the offal and hides for soup during a blockade; c) escalade; d) undermining the walls; e) sending down prisoners and loot.

storehouses of a castle might be, there must come a time when the food runs out, and if no assistance can penetrate the besieger's lines then the castle must yield, no matter how strong its defences or numerous its defenders. The same applies to a walled town or city, with the added burden of feeding a large number of non-combatants.

CHAPTER SEVEN

Heraldry

SOLDIERS were painting decorative insignia on their
shields as long ago as 2000 B.C., in the armies of the
Pharaohs, and from that date until today fighting men have
almost always borne some form of insignia on their person
or on their weapons, horses, or fighting vehicles. The Phry-
gians of Asia Minor, the ancient Greeks and Macedonians,
the Etruscans, Romans, Gauls, Picts and Britons, Byzantines, Vikings, Saxons and Angles, Normans, and even the
Saracens – all used devices on their shields and banners,
devices similar to those found in heraldry, such as animals,
birds, fish, heavenly bodies, geometric and floral designs.
The purpose of these insignia was to identify the bearer in
battle, promote an *esprit de corps* and, in the case of the
leader's flag, to provide a spearhead for an attack, a focal
point for a defence and a rallying point in the confusion of a
mêlée. These devices were used successfully for centuries,
so what made the Frankish system now known as heraldry
necessary, and different? Why should it warrant a rigid set
of rules governing the use of certain insignia, and cause the
evolution of heralds to interpret, and the founding of

Colleges of Arms to record and issue, those insignia? The answer is that, unlike their predecessors, heraldic insignia were hereditary.

Flags had been used by the Franks to identify a feudal lord and his followers in battle since the time of Charlemagne. The insignia on these banners were not hereditary, often being changed several times within the lifetime of the bearer, so why, even if a definite system of insignia was necessary, did it become essential to make such insignia hereditary? There were two main reasons. Firstly, towards the end of the eleventh century the tournament became very popular in France and during the next fifty years spread throughout Europe to become a major pastime of the nobility. Rules were introduced as the sport developed and one of these was that combatants should wear a coat over their armour so that spectators might recognise them easily; recognition being a problem because a lord's banner was never carried on his tourney lance. (Heraldry is usually associated with the shield but it should be pointed out that in medieval times the lance pennon or banner was more easily recognisable at a distance and was therefore far more important on the battlefield than shield markings, and the heraldic flag had no place in civil life until the end of the fifteenth century.) For the tourney, therefore, the insignia on a lord's shield was repeated on a coat worn over the armour, and this gave rise to the term 'coat of arms' or 'coat armour.' Strolling players acted as masters of ceremony at the tournaments, identifying knights by their insignia and announcing their names and titles to the spectators, and this encouraged knights seeking glory in the tourney always to use the same insignia. The second reason was that at the end of the eleventh century the Crusades began and for the first time the chivalry of Europe came together; scores of kings and princes, hundreds of barons. Obviously it was necessary that the various leaders and their followers should be easily recognisable. They already bore banners for identification, the insignia repeated on the lord's shield, but there was a great deal of duplication of insignia amongst knights from the different countries and it became essential that some regulating system be established to ensure that unique coats of arms were allocated to at least the greater barons. However, the establishment of a recognised system of insignia did not cause it to become hereditary: this was due to the barons having their distinctive insignia inscribed on their great seals, which were used, in those days of general illiteracy, to authenticate documents; and on their seal rings, which were recognised as representing the authority of the lord and were often loaned to trusted messengers or captains to assist them in carrying out missions on behalf of their lord.

The choice of insignia and the formation of the rules of heraldry came about primarily through the sharing of knowledge of existing coats of arms between the strolling players, or heralds as they were referred to by the last quarter of the twelfth century. Certainly by the end of the century these heralds could recognise knights by their banners and shields, not only in their own countries, but also in most countries of western Europe. The value of such men was soon recognised by army commanders and it became customary for a herald to be always close to the commander to assist in identifying the various contingents of the army for deployment and to recognise an enemy's strength and dispositions by identifying his banners. A great lord advertising his presence by his banner could inspire confidence in the troops around him, but he might also attract an unwelcome concentration of enemies, intent on taking him to cause the downfall of his followers, or for his value in the form of ransom, and ruses were therefore employed to confuse observers, especially in the case of a king leading an army in battle. At the battle of Poitiers, for example, there were no less than twenty kings of France on the field.

By 1300 heraldry had developed into an intricate science with the distinctive hereditary insignia painted not only on

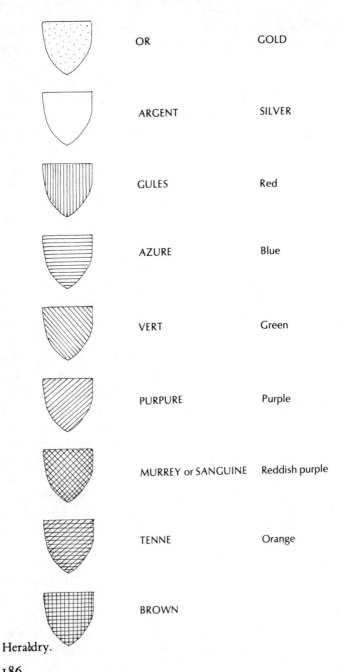

	OR	GOLD
	ARGENT	SILVER
	GULES	Red
	AZURE	Blue
	VERT	Green
	PURPURE	Purple
	MURREY or SANGUINE	Reddish purple
	TENNE	Orange
	BROWN	

Heraldry.

fighting men's banners, shields and surcoats, but also on their horses' trappers, their ailettes and helmet crests. It is not generally realised that by this date the burghers and even the peasants of some Continental countries had adopted arms also. This was certainly the case in Portugal and Germany, while in France the bourgeoisie were bearing arms as early as the first quarter of the thirteenth century, the peasantry by *c.* 1370. Indeed, the science was at its height during the fourteenth and most of the fifteenth centuries, but in the last quarter of the fifteenth century it began a gradual decline, losing its original purpose of the identification of individuals and their followers in battle, and assuming instead a largely decorative role. Because of the complexity of this later form of heraldry, brought about by the bearing of arms by all and sundry, many people believe the subject to be immensely complicated. This is far from the truth, for originally heraldry was designed to enable men to be recognised by simple, clear symbols, and was based upon a number of very straightforward rules. Once these are explained heraldry in the medieval period is easy to understand, but first it is necessary to learn a few basic heraldic terms.

The Shield

The front of the shield is known as the field or ground. In order to describe exactly whereabouts on the field the various symbols should be placed it is divided into nine points. These are shown in the figure on page 190: A dexter chief; B middle chief; C sinister chief; D honour point; E fess point; F nombril point; G dexter base; H middle base; I sinister base. When looking at the shield the dexter side is on the left, the sinister on the right, because

(Left) The shading always used to represent metals and colours. Modern heralds sometimes use solid black for Sable in published material, and Sable is shown thus in this book; the hatching for Sable being used for Brown instead.

although dexter means right and sinister left, the shield points are named from the knight's position behind his shield.

Tinctures

The various colours used for the field and the devices painted upon it are all known as tinctures. There are three classes: metals, colours and furs. The metals are gold (*Or*), and silver (*Argent*); the colours are red (*Gules*), blue (*Azure*), black (*Sable*), green (*Vert*), and purple (*Purpure*). Two other colours are used less frequently: *Murrey*, sometimes called *Sanguine*, which is a mulberry colour; and *Tenné*, which is orange. These two colours are found mainly in Continental heraldry, though they do appear occasionally on English flags or as livery colours. *Russet* is also found occasionally in Continental heraldry and occurs in English heraldry on the flags and liveries of the great Percy family. Commoners in Portugal were not allowed to use metals.

Furs were originally just *Ermine* and *Vair* but the increase in the number of coats of arms during the fourteenth and fifteenth centuries led to variants of these being introduced. *Ermine* is represented by black spots on a white field; *Vair* is always *Azure* and *Argent* unless otherwise stated, when it is known as *Vairé*. For example, *Vairé*, *Or* and *Gules*, the coat of the Ferrers, Earls of Derby. The variants for *Ermine* are: *Ermines* (white spots on black); *Erminois* (black spots on gold); and *Pean* (gold spots on black.) For *Vair* they are: *Vair en Point*, *Counter-Vair*, *Potent*, and *Counter-Potent*. All these varieties of *Vair* are *Azure* and *Argent* unless stated otherwise.

In Spanish and Portuguese heraldry only *Ermine* and *Vair* are used. In French and Italian heraldry there occasionally appear further variants known as *Plumeté* and *Papelonné*. These are illustrated by the arms of Tenremonde of Brabant and Monti of Florence respectively.

ERMINE

VAIR

COUNTER-VAIR

VAIR-EN-POINT

COUNTER-POTENT

POTENT

The Furs

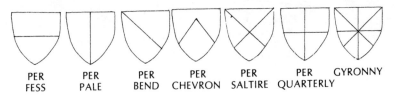

PER FESS · PER PALE · PER BEND · PER CHEVRON · PER SALTIRE · PER QUARTERLY · GYRONNY

Divisions of the Field

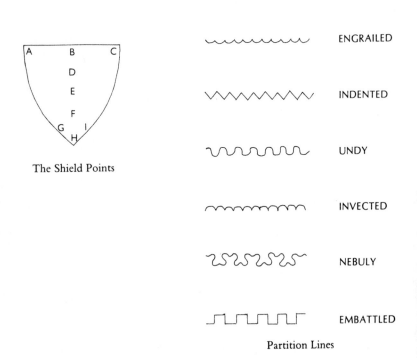

The Shield Points

ENGRAILED

INDENTED

UNDY

INVECTED

NEBULY

EMBATTLED

Partition Lines

Rule of Tincture

The rule of tincture is one of the most ancient and important rules of heraldry. It states that a colour must never be placed upon a colour, nor a metal upon a metal. There are several permitted exceptions to the rule, such as the claws and tongue of an animal, or a canton or chief added to a coat as a sign of honour, but most exceptions are a violation of the rule, perhaps caused by ignorance on the part of the painter or misinterpretation of faded colours by later copyists.

Divisions of the Shield

The shield may be divided by a line or lines and a field thus divided is described as parted or party. There are seven main divisions of this nature, illustrated by the accompanying figures.

Continental heraldry contains many other divisions, which are unknown in Britain. One of the most common, especially in Germany and Italy, is a tripartite division of the field by two lines running horizontally, vertically or diagonally across the field. These are known as *tierced in fess* (Counts von Zedwitz of Bohemia), *tierced in pairle* (the Saxon family of von Briesen), and *tierced in bend* (the Nompar family of Guyenne – formerly known as Aquitaine.) Another curious partition, unique to Germany, is *tierced in gyron gyronnant* (von Megenzer.)

Some other divisions of the field found in Continental heraldry are *Mantelé*, *Chapé* and *Chaussé*. These differ from other parted fields in that any charges which appear on one section of the field do not extend to the other sections. *Mantelé* may be seen in the arms of the Ghisi family of Venice, and *Chapé* in the arms of the de Hauten family of Burgundy. *Chaussé* is the reverse of *Chapé*. When the *Chapé* or *Chaussé* is formed by an arched or concave line it is said to be *ployé*, as in the arms of von Schleich of Bavaria. Three tinctures are often used for this and for *Mantelé*. *Chaperonné* is a term applied to the *Chapé* when it does not extend beyond the *Fess* line.

Partition Lines

To provide more coats of arms irregular partition lines were introduced. Originally there were only three varieties:

Engrailed, Indented or Dancetty, and Undy or Wavy. Invected, Nebuly and Embattled were added later. These are shown in the figure on page 190. There were many more varieties but these are unlikely to have been used, or to have been in general use, before 1500.

Shield charges: Honourable Ordinaries

From the earliest days of heraldry shields were 'charged' with various devices, such as the lions of the Normans, the eagle of the Holy Roman Empire, and the fleurs-de-lis of France. Obviously plain colours, or several colours on a divided field, could not provide all the variations needed to make coats of arms unique and therefore a series of charges were used on the fields. The term Ordinary is given to those simple emblems which were amongst the first to be so used, and of these Ordinaries the nine most ancient and important ones are known as the Honourable Ordinaries. They are the Chief (Ducs de Montferrat); Fess (Ducs de Bouillon); Pale (Barons Skrbensky de Hrzistic of Silesia); Chevron (Comtes de Sart from the Low Countries); Bend (Count Thun de Hohenstein of Bohemia); Saltire (van Eyck of the Low Countries); Cross (Republic of Genoa); Pile (the Lords Chandos); and Quarter (Count Waldersee of Prussia.)

Some of the Honourable Ordinaries have diminutive forms. Only the more commonly used ones have been listed here.

FESS. Bar, half the breadth of the Fess and rarely used singly: Closet, half the breadth of the Bar: Barrulet, half the breadth of the Closet: Barry (Gonzagas, Dukes of Mantua), a series of Barrulets, always exceeding five and used only in even numbers. (If the divisions of the field are very numerous, say ten or more, it is referred to as Barruly.) The Fess Arched is a variant found only in Continental heraldry (Balbi-Porto family of Venice.) Another Continental variant is the Spanish Campada, where the 'Fess' is placed at

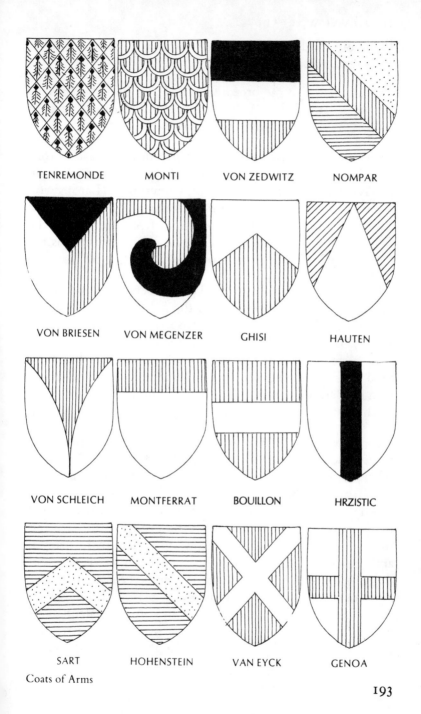

TENREMONDE   MONTI   VON ZEDWITZ   NOMPAR

VON BRIESEN   VON MEGENZER   GHISI   HAUTEN

VON SCHLEICH   MONTFERRAT   BOUILLON   HRZISTIC

SART   HOHENSTEIN   VAN EYCK   GENOA

Coats of Arms

the base of the shield. Bars-gemels is a term given to Barrulets or Closets placed in pairs.

PALE. Pallet, half the breadth of the Pale: Endorse, half the breadth of the Pallet: Paly (Stübner of Austria), a series of Pallets, used in the same manner as Barry.

CHEVRON. Chevronnel, half the breadth of the chevron: Couple-close, half the breadth of the Chevronnel and always borne double or more: Chevronny (Barons von Bussnang), applied in the same manner as Barry: Chevron couché, in which the Chevron issues from the side of the field, is sometimes found in Continental heraldry, as is the Chevron reversed (Barons Rumlingen de Berg of Bavaria.)

BEND. Bendlet, half the breadth of the Bend: Riband, never more than one-sixth the area of the field and usually borne each side of a Bend like a Cotise (see below). When a Riband or Cotise is cut short at the ends, known as couped, it is called a Baston or Baton. Bendy, a series of Bendlets, used as Barry and Paly, as in the arms of the Fieschi of Genoa. Bendy sinister, as Bendy but running from top right of the field.

PILE. There are no diminutives of the Pile but sometimes three Piles are used together (Lord Basset of Drayton), when they normally issue from the Chief but may also issue from the base or sides of the field.

Paly, Bendy, Barry and Chevronny are known as varied fields. More complex fields may be produced by crossing the lines: Barry-Bendy, a division of the field by horizontal and diagonal lines; Paly-Bendy, with the lines vertical and diagonal; and Checky, horizontal and vertical lines; but none of these were common in our period. Both Barry-Bendy and Paly-Bendy have their sinister equivalents. The varied fields may also be varied again by the use of irregular partition lines, such as Barry nebuly, the arms of the Ducs de Mortemar in France.

CHANDOS

WALDERSEE

GONZAGAS

BALBI-PORTO

STÜBNER

VON BUSSNANG

BERG

FIESCHI

BASSET

MORTEMAR

AUSTIN

LATIMER

VOLZ

RADA

PIERREFEU

TOULOUSE

CROSS. There are a great number of forms of cross in medieval heraldry but there is room here to show only a few of the main types. Those illustrated are: Cross Passant (Austin of Norfolk); Cross Patoncée (Latimer of England); Cross Patée or Formée (Volz of Bavaria); Cross Flory (Rada of Spain); Cross Botonnée (Pierrefeu of France); Cross Pomel, Pomettée or Bourdonée (Comtes de Toulouse); Cross Potent (Dukes of Calabria); Cross Crosslet (Beauchamp, Earls of Warwick); Cross Moline (Villehardouin of France); Cross Fourchée (de Kulenthal of Germany); Voided or False Cross (de Crevecoeur of Normandy).

Any cross is termed Quadrate if its limbs project from a square in the centre. If the lower limb of a cross tapers to a point it is described as Fitchée; for example, Patée Fitchée.

Subordinate Ordinaries

The Subordinate Ordinaries are the twelve less important charges of ancient origin. Many of these are only borne in multiples. Pairle or Pall (Deichsler of Bavaria); Fret (Maltravers of England); Lozenge (Counts of Schwerin); Mascle (Merseman of Flanders); Rustre (Soumeret d'Essenau of Flanders); Fusil (Counts von Egger of Austria); Orle (Bertram of England); Tressure (Sir John Chidiok of England); Gyron (Giron of Spain); Checky (de Warenne, Earls of Surrey); Flanches (Martinet of Spain); and Roundels (Medici, Grand Dukes of Tuscany.) Some of these are known by different names when used in multiples: Fretty, Lozengy, Masculy, Fusily and Gyronny. The Tressure is often decorated with fleurs-de-lis and this is described as a tressure flory. When a double tressure has fleurs-de-lis pointing outwards and inwards alternately it is known as a double tressure flory-counter-flory, as in the arms of the kings of Scotland.

Roundels are given different names for each colour or metal: Bezants (*Or*); Plates (*Argent*); Hurts (*Azure*); Tor-

CALABRIA   BEAUCHAMP   CREVECOEUR   VILLEHARDOUIN

KULENTHAL   DEICHSLER   MALTRAVERS   SCHWERIN

MERSEMAN   d'ESSENAU   VON EGGER   BERTRAM

CHIDIOK   GIRON   WARENNE   MARTINET

teaux (*Gules*); Pellets (*Sable*); and Pomeis (*Vert*). They may also be shown as furs, when they use the name of that fur, or may bear wavy lines running across them horizontally (Barry-wavy) when they are known as Fountains and are always *Argent* and *Azure*. (The arms of the Wells family of England.)

Animate and Inanimate Charges

Various animals were used as distinctive charges from the beginning and the development of the Honourable and Subordinate Ordinaries was therefore paralleled by the development of a whole range of charges based on animate and inanimate objects. A list of the more common charges is given below, and as many have been illustrated as this book provides room for.

Although by their very nature these charges are more complex than the Ordinaries, it will be noticed from the examples that they are still very simple in design. This was because there were accepted methods of portraying each charge, the heraldic lion, for example, being a stylised animal which bears little resemblance to the real lion, though its stylisation does provide uniformity and instant recognition of the device. Similarly it will be noted that tinctures remain very plain, the most popular being *Or*, *Argent*, *Gules* and *Azure*, with occasionally *Sable* and less frequently *Ermine* or *Vair*.

BEASTS. Lions, bears, boars, bulls, foxes, stags and wolves. These were portrayed in a number of different stances: Lion rampant (Counts of Flanders); Lion passant (Nicholas Carew of Ireland); and Lion passant regardant (the arms of England from 1154–1340). The heads of these animals were also used as charges.

BIRDS. Eagles, alerions (eagles without beaks and claws); chough, corbie or raven, martlet or swallow (always shown

MEDICI	SCOTLAND	WELLS	FLANDERS
CAREW	ENGLAND 1154–1340	LORRAINE	POLAND
RAVENTHORPE	ARUNDEL	DAUPHIN OF FRANCE	RAINEVAL
BARRE	GRIFFA	GRANULLAS	CORTI

without feet and beak), and parrots. The Holy Roman Empire used a single-headed eagle displayed (as in the arms of the kings of Poland, 1255–1385, but *Sable* eagle on *Or* field) until *c.* 1376. The double-headed eagle may have been used after that date, but the first definite reference for the double-headed eagle is 1414, after which date the single-headed eagle became the emblem of the King of the Romans. An alerion is shown in the arms of the Dukes of Lorraine; a raven in Raventhorpe of England; and martlets in Sir John Arundel, 1418–1483.

FISH. Dolphin (arms of the Dauphins of France from 1343); barbel (Comte de Barre), escallop (Waleran de Raineval, Comte de Fauquembergues), and pike or salmon.

MONSTERS. Griffin (Griffa of Naples).

HUMAN BODY. Eyes (Granullas of Catalonia); hands; arms; legs; hearts (Corti of Spain); heads.

HEAVENLY BODIES. Crescents (Togores of Spain); stars; suns.

VEGETABLE KINGDOM. Fleurs-de-lis (Florence); rose (Sir William Vaux, 1437–1471); cinquefoil (Sir William Motton, 1430–1482); chaplet or garland (Ralph FitzWilliam of England, fourteenth century); garb or wheatsheaf (Earls of Chester).

ARTIFICIAL OBJECTS (Military). Arrows; axes, broad arrows (Earl of Leicester); caltraps (Trappe of England); castles or towers; gonfannons (Comtes d'Auvergne); helmets; ladders; shields; swords.

ARTIFICIAL OBJECTS (Civil). Annulets or rings (Lowther); billets (Anvin of Picardy); bourdons (Steps of the Low Countries); breys (de Geneville of France); buckles; chains;

TOGORES   FLORENCE   VAUX   MOTTON

FITZWILLIAM   CHESTER   LEICESTER   TRAPPE

AUVERGNE   LOWTHER   ANVIN   STEPS

GENEVILLE   CLEEVES   VAN DER HOVEN   MAGALOTTI

chess rooks; clarion; escarbuncles (Comtes de Cleeves); hammers; horseshoes (van der Hoven of Holland); letters of the alphabet (Magalotti of Florence); maunche or sleeve (Hastings, Earls of Huntingdon); mullet or spur (Lord de Wigtown, fourteenth century); water budget or bucket (Trusbutts, Barons of Wartre in Yorkshire.)

RUNIC CHARGES. Medieval Polish heraldry made use of charges of a runic nature, all the Polish nobility being believed to be of Scandinavian origin. Most common of these symbols were those resembling arrows (the emblem of Thor), stars and crescents, as in the coats of the Sapieha, Sas and Leliwa families.

Differencing

The earliest coats of arms tended to be simple, often a plain field in a colour or metal, with perhaps an animal or an Ordinary upon it. As more people adopted arms it was natural for those families who were related to each other, or who owed allegiance to a great lord under the feudal system, to use the simple arms of their relatives or superiors, adding some other charge, or parting or varying the field, to produce their own distinctive arms. Thus early coats of arms not only distinguished the bearer, but also often showed to whom he was related and/or to whom he owed allegiance. This method of varying arms was known as Differencing.

A good example of Differencing occurs with the English family of Lutterell which, in the first half of the fourteenth century, bore *Azure*, a bend between six martlets *Or*. The de Furnivals, who held their lands by feudal tenure under the Lutterells, bore *Argent*, a bend between six martlets *Gules*. The de Ecclesall family, sub-tenants in turn to the de Furnivals, bore *Sable*, a bend between six martlets *Or*.

In Continental heraldry the most common methods of Differencing were a different helmet crest (see below) for

HASTINGS WIGTOWN TRUSBUTTS LUTTERELL

SAPIEHA SAS LELIWA PARTENECK

DE VERE GREY DUNBAR PARR

SOMERSET ELTHAM GEOFFROI
DE BRABANT WILLIAM IV
OF MELUN

each branch of a family or a variation of field and charge tinctures as described above. The Bavarian family of Parteneck, for example, bore *Argent*, an axe-head *Sable*, while other branches of the family bore *Argent*, an axe-head *Gules* (Cammer); *Gules*, an axe-head *Argent* (Cammerberg); *Or*, an axe-head *Azure* (Hilgertshauser) and *Azure*, an axe-head *Or* (Massenhauser). In all these branches the small maltese cross on the axe-blade was *Sable*.

Cadency

Cadency is the name given to the system for distinguishing between the arms of the father and his sons. There were various systems employed in the early days of heraldry, for which there do not appear to have been any common rulings on usage, and those still in use during the 1300–1500 period are detailed below.

THE BORDURE. The bordure was employed as a mark of cadency from the earliest times, different tinctures or irregular partition lines serving to identify the various members of a family. This is shown by the arms of the de Veres, Earls of Oxford. In our illustration the arms have a bordure indented to signify the arms are those of the earl's younger son. This method is the most common in Spanish and Portuguese heraldry, other methods being almost unknown, but is rarely found in German arms. It continued to be used as a difference after other systems had been invented and accepted.

SEMÉE. In this system diminutive forms of charges were repeated on the field and examples exist of the fleur-de-lis, roundel, crescent, chaplet, escallop, cinquefoil, rose, billet, annulet, mullet, martlet and various forms of cross all being employed for this purpose. Semée gave rise to the diminutives becoming very numerous so as to form a patterned field. These are referred to as crusily for the cross, billety for billets, bezanty for bezants, and so on. A semée of fleurs-de-lis is known as semée-de-lis. Where no such terms can be applied, as with the escallop and cinquefoil, this is known as a semée of . . .

GERATTYNG. Under this sytem only nine diminutive charges were employed as marks of cadency for the sons, most often used singly on the principle charge of the family arms. In sequence these nine charges are: small crosses or crosslets of Cross Patée, Cross Fleury, or Cross Crosslet, sometimes Fitchée; Fleur-de-lis; Roses; Primroses – probably Quatrefoils; Cinquefoils; Escallops; Chaplets; Mullets and Crescents. Gerattyng continued to be used until *c.* 1350.

THE BEND. The bend was a common form of cadency mark in the thirteenth century, placed over the paternal arms, and was still in general use up to about 1325. An example appears in the arms of John de Grey, son of Lord Grey, both of whom were present at the siege of Caerlaverock in Scotland in 1300.

THE LABEL. In this system the heir bears his father's arms differenced with crosslets, or one of the other diminutive charges; the second son bears his father's arms with a label of three points (the first point represents the father, the second the heir, and the third the second son) as in the arms of Patrick Dunbar, son of the Earl of Dunbar, in the fourteenth century. The third son bears his father's arms with a label of four points and so on. The heir would abandon the difference on the death of his father, and *his* sons would then bear the marks described above. The sons of the second son bore differences as follows: first son, father's arms with a label and a difference; second son, father's arms with a label and a bordure; third son, father's arms with a bordure of a different tincture; all further sons the father's arms with bordures of various tinctures.

From about 1350 the marks of cadency in English

heraldry have been: first son, label; second son, crescent; third son, mullet; fourth son, martlet; fifth son, annulet; sixth son, fleur-de-lis; seventh son, rose; eighth son, cross moline; ninth son, double quatrefoil. The crescent is shown as a mark of cadency on the arms of Sir John Parr, 1438–1475.

CONTINENTAL SYSTEMS. European countries also tried various methods of cadency, but none of these evolved into a permanent and complete system as in England. The main methods employed were: 1) father's arms in different tinctures. 2) Multiplication of a charge, i.e. if a coat has a martlet for a charge the sons use two, three, four martlets, and so on. 3) Addition of a charge inherited from mother or wife. 4) A different crest for each son, except in Polish heraldry where all nobles wore the same style crest – three ostrich feathers. 5) Quartering of the arms with those of wife or mother.

Illegitimacy

In the period with which we are dealing the bastards of kings and princes were proud of their parentage and had the right to bear arms *similar* to the royal arms. The most common form of differencing the father's arms was the Baton, a narrow bar placed across the arms, as in the arms of Charles Somerset, Earl of Worcester, bastard of the third Duke of Somerset. The Baton is usually couped, i.e. not touching the sides of the field. In England since the fifteenth century the Baton has been allocated to illegitimate descendants of the Royal Family only.

Other methods of indicating illegitimacy include 1). Father's arms in different tinctures. 2). Charges of the father's arms rearranged to form a different coat. 3). A bend bearing the father's arms placed over the bastard's own coat. 4). A charge of the father's arms set on a new field.

In Continental heraldry the bend sinister is a mark of

illegitimacy if used over the other bearings. In France the paternal arms were used but with the charges facing the sinister side, all charges normally facing the dexter side.

Augmentation

Augmentations are additional charges granted by a sovereign as special marks of favour or honour in reward for valour or extraordinary service. The method does not appear in English heraldry until after about 1375.

An augmentation might be a canton added to the dexter chief, an entire chief added to the arms, quartering of the arms with those of the sovereign, or might even entail the adoption of a new coat of arms. For example, the Châteaubriand family, who bore *Gules*, semée de pommes de pin d'*Or*, were granted permission to wear *Gules*, semée de lis d'*Or* by Louis IX in reward for the valour of a member of the family at Mansourah in 1250.

Marshalling

Marshalling is the arranging of two or more coats of arms on one shield to indicate an alliance, either of marriage or estates. As with differencing and cadency, several methods preceded the final one – quartering – which was introduced in the last quarter of the thirteenth century.

The earliest form of illustrating an alliance between two families or lordships was called compounding arms and consisted of taking the principal charges from each coat and blending them to form a new coat. Another early method was that known as the charged bordure, in which a bordure of the allied arms was added, as in the arms of John of Eltham, Earl of Cornwall and son of Edward II, who used the arms of England, with a bordure of France for his mother. A third method, still in use in the fourteenth century, was that known as dimidiation, in which the dexter half of one coat overlapped the sinister half of the other. A husband's arms were always on the dexter side and were not precisely halved, although the wife's were: see the arms of Geoffroi de Brabant, son of the Duke of Brabant, whose mother was Alice of Burgundy. Geoffroi bore the arms of Brabant impaling those of Burgundy. This could give rise to some clumsy designs and the method was soon replaced by Impaling in which each coat was precisely halved. Impalement was not as a rule a permanent combination of the arms and the children of the marriage inherited only their father's arms.

Quartering came into being in the last quarter of the thirteenth century and was originally used to show alliances between kingdoms, but it was soon adopted by nobles to indicate a union between lordships, whereas dimidiation and impalement were used almost entirely for the union of marriage, especially from the late fourteenth century.

In quartering, the field is divided into four equal parts, numbered 1 top left, 2 top right, 3 bottom left, 4 bottom right. An example of quartering is given in the arms of William IV of Melun, Constable of Normandy, who fought at Agincourt.

Helmet Crests

Helmet crests are not necessarily linked with the charges borne on the wearer's shield, beasts and birds being particular favourites regardless of the charges on the shield. However, the colours employed for these crests were usually the same as the principal colours of the arms.

Crests were very popular in Germany, England and the Low Countries, but were seldom worn in France, Italy and Portugal. In Spain they were almost unknown, even amongst the greatest families. French peasants and bourgeoisie bearing arms were not allowed crests. As mentioned earlier, all Polish crests consisted of three ostrich feathers.

Crests were made of parchment, whalebone, plumes and feathers, wood, papier mâché and *cuir bouilli*, the latter

KING OF FRANCE COMTE DE NAMUR DU GUESCLIN DUC de BOURGOGNE

DUC de ANJOU MARECHAL DE CLERMONT MASTINO DELLA SCALA DUC DE SAVOY

HOLY ROMAN EMPEROR UNTIL 1400 MARGRAVE DE BRANDENBURG DUC de BAVARIA DUC DE SAXE

Coats of Arms and Crests

being one of the most popular materials because it was strong yet light. The feathers came from cockerels, swans and peacocks and were usually arranged as a panache, i.e. rising in tiers to a point, or as a plume, in which only one or two tiers were used. They were occasionally dyed in the principal tinctures of the wearer's arms.

The crest began to go out of fashion early in the fifteenth century, except at tournaments.

Scarf and Wreath

The scarf was a short piece of cloth, in the tinctures of the wearer's arms, which protected the helmet from the rusting effect of damp and the wearer of that helmet from the roasting effect of the sun. It first appears in general use in the early fourteenth century. It was replaced *c.*1350 by the wreath, a ring made of two skeins of silk or other material in the tinctures of the wearer's arms, twisted together. The crest was laced or bolted to the helmet and the wreath was attached to the base of the crest to conceal this joint. A chapeau, a cap of scarlet fur with an ermine turn-up, was worn instead of a wreath by high ranking nobles. After about 1380 a coronet was worn by dukes, princes and kings.

Surcoats and Jupons

By the beginning of the fourteenth century surcoats usually bore the heraldic devices of their wearers. It was normal for these surcoats to be in the principal colour or metal of the arms with the principal charge on the breast and back, and sometimes on the front of the skirt (one each side of the central slit), but occasionally an entire coat of arms might be reproduced instead of a single charge.

When the surcoat was replaced by the jupon *c.*1350–1360 the method of wearing arms on the garment also changed, the coat of arms now being reproduced over the entire front

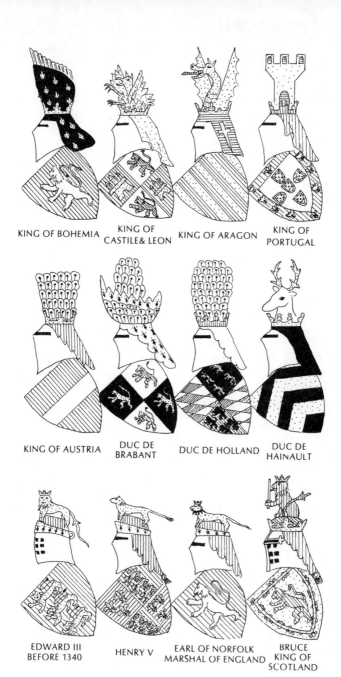

KING OF BOHEMIA

KING OF
CASTILE & LEON

KING OF ARAGON

KING OF
PORTUGAL

KING OF AUSTRIA

DUC DE
BRABANT

DUC DE HOLLAND

DUC DE
HAINAULT

EDWARD III
BEFORE 1340

HENRY V

EARL OF NORFOLK
MARSHAL OF ENGLAND

BRUCE
KING OF
SCOTLAND

of the jupon as if on a shield, and repeated thus on the back, the two divided by the side lacing.

The jupon was discarded *c.*1425 and for some time armour was as a general rule uncovered, being known as 'white' armour. Occasionally examples occur of knights having their arms engraved and gilded on the breastplate but this was a comparatively rare occurrence. The tabard, a short, loose garment, open at the sides and with broad, short sleeves, began to appear from about 1425 and coats of arms continued to be embroidered on these or on cloaks, but both these garments were more for the tournament than for warfare, or for the non-combatant heralds, who wore their master's coat. The tabard became more popular at the end of the century.

Badges

The use of badges to identify the followers of a lord became widespread in the second half of the fifteenth century, but badges had been used to a lesser degree in the previous century, mainly by the kings, princes and great nobles. These badges took two distinctive forms; the personal badge of the lord, which could only be used by him but which was not normally worn on his person in the 1300–1500 period, and the household badge which was used on the tunics of servants, dependants, retainers and followers, who had no arms of their own and no right to bear the arms of their lord. The household badge is therefore a mark of allegiance and is generally but not always different from the charges of the lord's coat of arms. Such badges were widely displayed on liveries, flags and property and were therefore far more widely known by the ordinary people than the arms of the lord, which were only displayed on the lord's person, his lance pennon and banner. In battle a lord's followers and retainers wore the household badge on their clothes and rallied round a standard or banner bearing that same badge. The badges are variously described as being worn on the shoulder or on the sleeve, but certainly by the fifteenth century the most common position was on the breast.

A badge was usually only granted by a sovereign to those nobles who could field a large following. The granting of a badge was always accompanied by the grant of a standard, guidon or badge-pennon, for the badge was used instead of a coat of arms on the battle flag of a lord.

Badges were never so important in Europe as in England, and their use was never so widespread.

Liveries

A livery was a tunic worn by a servant or follower of a lord in the principal colour of that lord's arms and trimmed with the colour of the principal charge; these two colours being the livery colours. However, no heraldic rule governs precisely the choice of colours for liveries and some bore no relation to the coat of arms: the retainers of the Percy family of Northumberland, for example, wore *Russet* and *Tenné* with the golden lion rampant of the family arms on their shoulders, whereas the tinctures of the Percy arms were *Azure* and *Or*.

Yellow was normally worn instead of gold, white instead of silver. Red was reserved for royalty in England and any lord having red as his principal colour had to use a claret shade or a chocolate colour. Blue and green could be in any shade, at the lord's wish. For furs the colour of the ground was taken, i.e. white for Ermine, black for Pean and Ermines, yellow for Erminois.

Liveries were worn increasingly in the fourteenth century, becoming common by the fifteenth century, but there is evidence to suggest that some baronial retinues were dressed in the livery of their lord at a much earlier date, perhaps as early as the beginning of the thirteenth century. Thus we can be reasonably certain that the retinues of the nobles were in livery by the fourteenth century, the custom spreading to the knights during that century. The livery colours of

Edward I were white and red; of Edward III, mauve and red; of Henry V, white and blue. Those of the Dukes of Suffolk were blue and yellow; Oxford, red and yellow; the Earls of Douglas, blue and white; of Shrewsbury, red and yellow; of Warwick, red and white; of the Bohuns, Earls of Essex, blue and white. The livery colours of the House of Bourbon were white and green.

By the late fourteenth century the English appear to have adopted the red cross on a white background as a national livery, worn either as the livery or as a distinctive badge on the lord's livery. By the time of Agincourt, Henry V had made it compulsory for all members of his expedition to wear a large red cross on their chest and back. The French adopted a white cross as a national symbol, but this does not appear regularly in illustrations until *c.* 1450, by which time a national army had been formed. Both these crosses originate from the Third Crusade of 1189–1192. For this crusade the Germans wore yellow crosses and the Flemings green, but there is no evidence to suggest these colour distinctions were perpetuated as in the case of the English and French.

Horse Trappers

The basic colour of a trapper was normally the principal tincture of the rider's arms, with the principal charge repeated on each side of each half of the trapper. Where livery colours were different to the tinctures of the arms, these were sometimes used instead. As with surcoats, some trappers bore the entire coat of arms instead of just a charge.

The direction in which the charges should face needs a little clarification, owing to the emblems being worn on both sides of the horse. It would seem from examples studied that the horse's head was regarded as being on the dexter side and therefore on the mounted knight's left side the trapper bore the arms exactly as they appeared on the shield, but on the right hand side of the trapper the charges always faced in the opposite direction.

EDWARD I

EDWARD III

HENRY V

HENRY V

RICHARD DUKE
OF YORK

EDWARD, DUKE
OF YORK

TALBOT, EARL OF
SHREWSBURY

STAFFORD

DUKE OF CLARENCE

Livery Badges

Flags

By the fourteenth century flags had been categorised into seven main classes: pennoncelle, pennon, banner, standard, guidon, gonfannon and streamer, each of which had a definite size limit and, with the exception of the streamer, was allocated to men of a certain rank.

THE PENNONCELLE. The pennoncelle was the personal flag of all men-at-arms from the rank of knight up and was carried below the lance head. It took three main forms; a triangular flag known as the pavon, which was particularly popular during the fourteenth century; the swallow-tailed pennoncelle; and the single-tailed pennoncelle. In length the pennoncelle was between 12 and 18 in., the tails usually taking up at least half that length. The owner's arms were embroidered or painted on the material, often – but not always, so that the arms appeared the right way up only when the lance was lowered for the charge. During the fifteenth century it became customary for a badge on a livery colour to be used instead of the arms, and this was known as a badge pennoncelle.

THE PENNON. The pennon was a larger form of pennoncelle, taking the same three forms but measuring 2–3 ft. in length. It was the personal flag of a knight bachelor and was carried on his lance. As with the pennoncelle, a badge form was common in the fifteenth century. If a knight was promoted to banneret on the field of battle the tails of the pennon were cut off to convert it into a small banner.

THE BANNER. This was originally restricted to kings, princes, dukes, earls and barons but from at least 1350 it was also granted to those knights below the rank of peer who had valuable military experience, and these men became known as knights-banneret. The banner might be borne by its owner, or by a selected deputy, but it was never displayed

DUKES OF SUFFOLK

DUKES OF EXETER

COUNTS OF HAINAULT

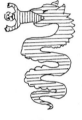

DUKES OF MILAN

DUKES OF SAVOY

DUKES OF
BRITTANY

HOUSE OF ORLEANS

HOUSE OF
BOURBON

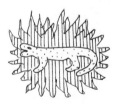

COUNTS OF
ANGOULEME

unless the owner was present, and then only if his forces
were arrayed for battle or actually advancing to the attack.

About 1300 most banners appear to have been rectangular in shape, 2–3 ft. deep by half that in width. Square
banners became predominant later, being 2–3 ft. square.
There was never any rule as to which shape should be used,

or exact measurements, but slightly smaller banners may have been used by those below the rank of peer. Like the previous two flags, the banner developed a badge form in the fifteenth century, although it was not common until the end of the century.

The banners of Continental peers often had a top edge which protruded beyond the vertical edge of the banner, and this was stiffened to keep the banner out straight. In German heraldry this extension is known as a Schwenkel and if it is red denotes a special privilege.

THE STANDARD. The standard was not a personal flag but was used to mark the position within an army of a body of men commanded by a great lord. It was never furled during a campaign but was used at the head of the force when on the march; at the group's headquarters when in camp; to lead assaults against the enemy; and to provide a rallying point – it bore the lord's badges, not his arms, and so bore the insignia worn by the men. During the 1300–1500 period the standard was granted only to peers and knights banneret.

The length of the standard was 6–12 feet. It was normally divided along its length into the tinctures of the owner's livery and charged with his badges, although charges from the arms were also used; rarely in England, as frequently as badges on the Continent. The national cross, St George for England, St Denis for France, etc., was usually carried in the hoist – the part of the flag nearest the staff – but Continental standards often bore the arms of the country here instead, or had no hoist compartment at all. English standards usually had a rounded end and if the end was split in two, these ends were also rounded. Continental standards frequently had split ends, which were pointed.

THE GUIDON. This was the cavalry equivalent of the standard, the latter being too long and unwieldy for mounted troops. It was 6–8 ft. long. The end was rounded (never split as in modern cavalry guidons.) The guidon was also

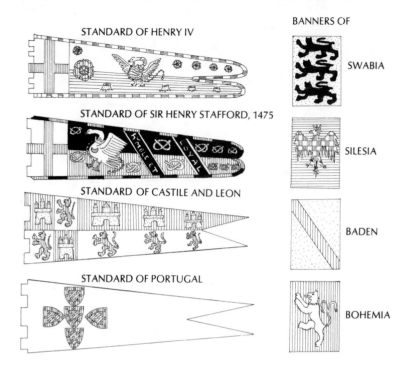

STANDARD OF HENRY IV

STANDARD OF SIR HENRY STAFFORD, 1475

STANDARD OF CASTILE AND LEON

STANDARD OF PORTUGAL

BANNERS OF

SWABIA

SILESIA

BADEN

BOHEMIA

divided into the hoist, containing the national cross or arms, and the livery colours charged with the owner's badges.

THE GONFANNON. The gonfannon was fixed to a horizontal bar suspended from a vertical staff. The lower edge often had several tassels or tails. It was carried by peers as an alternative to the banner and was used most often by those who held office in the Church or who took up arms on its behalf. It was especially common as a military banner in Italy, but was rare in England.

THE STREAMER. Streamer was the name given to the flag flown from the masthead of a ship, and followed the shapes of the single- or swallow-tailed pennon. In the second half of the fifteenth century such streamers were sometimes 40 yd. long and 8 yd. wide.

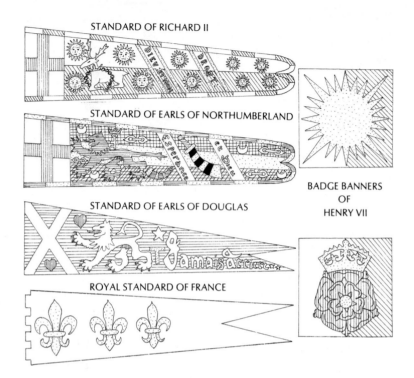

STANDARD OF RICHARD II

STANDARD OF EARLS OF NORTHUMBERLAND

STANDARD OF EARLS OF DOUGLAS

ROYAL STANDARD OF FRANCE

BADGE BANNERS
OF
HENRY VII

NATIONAL FLAGS. The national flags of England during our period were the banners of St Edmund, St Edward the Confessor, the Holy Trinity, Our Lady (a portrait of Mary), and the red cross of St George. These five banners were carried in every battle in which the kings of England were involved up to and including the battle of Bosworth in 1485. During the reign of Henry VII (1485–1509) St George became the recognised paramount saint of England and the other banners were discarded.

The first record of a royal banner occurs in 1301, when the banner of Edward I is described as three golden leopards 'running', on a red field. Later banners carried the royal coat of arms of the period.

The two principal flags of France in this period were the plain red banner of St Denis, the oriflamme, and the blue banner of St Martin with its semée of golden fleurs-de-lis,

220

reduced to three fleurs-de-lis after about 1365. Other early French flags often carry a white cross – the cross adopted by the French during the Crusades. Thus under the rule of Louis XI (1461–1483) the infantry bore scarlet flags bearing one or more white crosses. These were carried beside the fleurs-de-lis banner.

During the war with the Flemings in the early years of the fourteenth century many of the French guilds supplied men or hired mercenaries and these forces often had their own banners. For example, the locksmiths of La Rochelle had a scarlet banner bearing four golden keys; the metal workers of Laval a black banner bearing a silver hammer and files, and those of Niort a red banner bearing a silver cup with a golden fork and spoon on either side.

The national flag of Switzerland has been a white cross on a red field since 1339, but each canton marched under its own banner, most being simple designs of two colours, divided horizontally: St Gallen, green over white; Geneva, red over yellow; Aargau, black over blue; Berne, black over red; Fribourg, black over white; Lucerne, white over blue; Tessin, red over blue; Unterwalden, Solothurn and Obwalden, red over white. Glarus had three horizontal bars, red/black/red: Zurich, white over blue diagonally: Schwitz had a red banner with a small white cross in the top corner nearest the staff. Basel had a white flag with a black crozier head: Nidwalen, red over white with a double key motif: Schwyz, red with a gold canton depicting Christ on the cross in black: Uri, yellow with a black bull's head, eyes, nostrils and tongue in red: Appenzel, white with a black bear: Schaffhausen, a yellow banner with a black ram. The banners of Zurich and Basel had red schwenkels, that of Zurich bearing a white cross.

The national flag of the Holy Roman Empire was a black, double headed eagle on a gold field. The banners carried by the kings of Swabia, Silesia, Bohemia and Baden are illustrated in this chapter, as are some examples of Italian and Low Countries banners, and Spanish standards.

APPENDIX ONE

Modelling Medieval Soldiers

MANY readers will have put together a plastic construction kit at some time in their lives, and some will have explored the possibilities of conversion work on those kits. For those who are novices, what follows is a brief guide to the principal methods of converting model figures, together with some painting hints.

Conversion of a kit or ready-made figure can be as complicated or as simple as the modeller wishes, from a different 'paint job' or an interchange of parts between two or more kits, to a complete repositioning of the body and limbs. The important point to watch always is authenticity. By this I don't mean just the correct colours for painting, but that the body and limbs should be placed in realistic attitudes and that weapons, armour and clothing should be historically correct. Therefore, the first step before conversion begins is always research. (It is hoped this book will provide much of the information needed for the medieval period.)

Secondly you need a definite plan as to what your figure is doing – leaning nonchalantly on his spear, feeding his horse, practising archery at the butts, or kissing his sweetheart goodbye. Study pictures of horses, or real horses if possible, to see how the limbs bend, where the muscles show and how the coat catches the light. Do the same for human anatomy, either by buying a simple book on the subject or posing in front of a full-length mirror to see what angles can be achieved naturally at ankle, elbow, shoulder and so on. The 'How to Draw' series of small books is very useful at this stage.

In plastic modelling there are two main ways of repositioning limbs; the knife and heat. When using a knife a vee of plastic is taken from behind the joint to be bent, the limb repositioned at the required angle, then any remaining gaps filled with a piece of sprue and/or body putty. Green

Stuff or Plastic Padding make the best fillers. For the heat method the part to be changed can be held above the flame of a candle until it is soft enough for the position of the limb to be changed. Great care is needed here not to get too near the flame, nor to allow the plastic to get so hot that fine detail is lost elsewhere on the figure. Another method is the pyrogravure, a tool rather like a soldering iron which allows a very small but constant heat to pass through its metal tip. The tip is applied to the back of the joint, pressure applied on either side from the front, and the limb bent back to its new position.

Some parts of plastic kits are rather clumsy because of the limitations of the material in moulding, but these can soon be rectified to produce a more satisfactory figure. For example, weapons are frequently too thick for the scale, or too springy if thin. They can easily be replaced with wire, bladed or pointed weapons being made by flattening the wire in the right places and filing to the necessary shape or point. Micro strip can be used for belts and harness, and Micro rod cut across its width will provide buttons, and so on.

One of the most difficult things to get right is the creasing and folding of cloth. An early method was to use fine linen coated with a solution of plastic and carbon tetrachloride but this is now known to be a health hazard and dangerous except in the hands of experts, and simpler methods are now used. Paper can be cut into scale clothing and assembled just as in real life, crumpling the paper to break the grain and then smoothing it out again. Tissues are also useful and can be fixed to a figure in realistic folds and creases, then made permanent by the application of several layers of a thin, clear glue. Fine mesh stocking makes excellent mail once coated with silver paint. A good reference to all these aspects of plastic modelling, and many others besides, is *How to Go Plastic Modelling* by Chris Ellis, published by Patrick Stephens Ltd.

The same principles of construction and animation apply

to metal figures, except that different modelling materials are used. Modellers with experience of metal like to solder the parts of a kit together but this is best left to the experts and the modern five minute epoxy resins are perfectly adequate. Borden's Power Pack is recommended. A filler paste such as David's Isopon can also be used to join the parts, but in this case they need to be keyed – the flush surfaces criss-crossed with lines – to provide a secure join. The same applies to any gaps or holes which have to be filled after conversion work. Plastic Padding can also be used on keyed metal parts and may be filed and sanded to shape when hard. Thin sheet lead is often used to add clothing to metal figures being converted, or for shields and other extras. The metal foil from toothpaste tubes makes a good alternative and cooking foil can be used for very fine materials, such as lance pennons.

The more experienced modeller may like to 'scratch build' his figures. For this more advanced stage of the hobby high quality metal models of male nudes can be obtained from Rose Miniatures, 15 Llanover Road, London S.E.18. 3ST., or from Hinton Hunt Figures, Rowsley, River Road, Taplow, Bucks., to provide a basis on which to build. Some modellers make their own basic figures and J. G. Garratt's *Model Soldiers*, published by Seeley Service, describes how this is done. My own book *An Introduction to Battle Gaming*, published by Model and Allied Publications in 1972 (revised edition) has a short chapter on making lead soldiers, using your own plaster or silicone rubber moulds.

The crude metal figure is cut and bent to the attitude you require, using smooth jawed pliers to prevent marking the metal. The parts of the figure to be covered with other materials should then be keyed. As mentioned above, thin metal or lead sheet may be used for clothing and armour, but another perhaps easier method is to cover the figure with Polyfilla, made very stiff and put on thicker than will be required on the finished model. When the plaster has dried thoroughly, and this may take several days, it may be carved to the precise shapes needed, including such fine detail as head and facial hair. This method has the advantage that any mistakes or accidents can be easily rectified by adding more Polyfilla.

An important part of modelling any figure is the base on which the completed model will stand. Little extra touches may be added here to make a model more interesting and lifelike. The best reference for this stage is the series of articles which appeared monthly in *Airfix Magazine*, written by Roy Dilley, president of the British Model Soldier Society. Scenic flocks, artificial grass, sand, crushed earth, aggregate of the 3/8th to dust variety, all may be used to create a realistic surface for the figure to stand on, or even stone or cobble embossed plastic card could be used. These surfaces are cemented or glued to a piece of wood about 1 in. thick and of the appropriate area for the model, or you could use one of the smart plastic bases now produced by Bellona Ltd., or the wooden ones distributed by Historex Ltd.

A few extra touches such as grass from teased-out sisal string; rushes from old paint brush hairs; a 'rock' or two from the garden; a few sprigs of lichen for shrubbery; Polyfilla for mud, with the appropriate marks in it, and perhaps 'water' in some of the depressions, created with clear cement; all these touches go a long way towards making a good model excellent. In addition to *Airfix Magazine*, *Military Modelling* frequently runs long articles on this subject, and many ideas may be picked up from these articles and from the resulting readers' letters.

Painting

When painting a model figure it is advisable to mount it on a temporary stand so that the figure itself does not have to be fingered during the painting stage. This is best done by using an impact adhesive such as Evo-Stik to secure it to a length of thick dowel, which can be kept upright in a tin when not held in the hand, or to a cotton reel, which will stand up by itself. Horses will naturally need a wider surface to obtain good adhesion.

No undercoat is required for plastic figures, but if a great deal of conversion has been done it often helps to conceal the differences in texture between plastic and filler if a good coat of varnish is applied, or a coat of Unibond or similar white adhesive. This also seals body putty more effectively than paint. Before any paint is applied to a metal figure it should be given a little polish with a toothbrush to remove any bits, then with a softer brush, such as one of badger hair. If a metal or plastic figure has been assembled without any conversion it helps if it is washed in warm water to which a little detergent has been added: this removes any traces of grease deposited by your fingers during the modelling. Metal figures should then be given a thin undercoat, which will have an effect on the colours applied over it. White is normally used, but if there are to be some metal parts, as there obviously will be on most medieval figures, then black could be used for these areas, giving a more realistic shade to the silver paint applied over it. An alternative is to mix a little black or blue into the silver paint, using pure silver to highlight the metal. In my own opinion none of these methods gives a really satisfactory result and since metal figures have their own metal surfaces why not in these cases use the metal itself? Unfortunately many metal figures are supplied with their white undercoat already applied. This can be removed with paint stripper, always provided the figure is of pure metal and there are no areas or joins vulnerable to a chemical reaction. Flat surfaces can be scraped with a sharp knife blade and burnished by rubbing with a smooth piece of metal; a needle is handy here. Varnish will then give these parts a realistic finish. Alternatively the metal can be smoothed with very fine grade Wet and Dry abrasive paper and finished off with an abrasive liquid polish such as Brasso. Some people then cover the metal with black paint, wiping it off at once and leaving minimal amounts of black to outline any joints, ridges or engraving. Again seal with varnish.

A brief word here about brushes and paints. It is essential to buy the best brushes for good results – sable hair is the best; and to look after them so that they maintain their shape. Extremely small brushes can be bought, but these hold very little paint and do not give a good flow when trying to obtain a long straight line, and it is best to use sizes such as 3 and 4 rather than 0 and 1, except for the finest detail such as buttons, eyes, and so on. Type of paint is really a matter of personal taste; either oil-based paints such as the range of gloss and matt paints produced by Humbrol, or water based acrylics, which are similar to the ordinary household emulsion paint. Acrylic paints come in black, white, red, yellow and blue, and any colour or shade of colour can be made up from these. Naturally, a matt paint is more realistic for skin and textiles, and remember that in the medieval period dyes were of vegetable origin and were limited to greens, browns, dull reds and yellows or unbleached cloth for the ordinary people, bright red and purple being very expensive and used only by the rich.

Because of the size of the model and the great deal of fine detail on it, it is always best to apply the smallest amount of paint possible. Avoid too much brushing on plastic figures as this will 'lift' the paint. The flesh–coloured areas should be painted first, using a mix of white, yellow, red and brown until the correct shade is obtained. Add a little red to areas such as the ears, nostrils and lips and blend this into the flesh colour. Shade round the eyes with a light brown, a slightly darker shade at the bridge of the nose, under the nose, cheekbones, chin and lower lip and at the temples. Blend all this into the basic colour. Highlights of white should be on the ridge of the nose, sides of the nostrils, chin and cheekbones under the eyes, again all blended in. The eyes are probably the most difficult part of all. One method is to shade the whole eye socket a faint mauve, then draw a dark brown line for the upper eyelid and add the iris and pupil below this. Close up this looks rather artificial, but from the normal viewing distance it is quite effective. Another method is to paint a white area for the eyeball, not too large, and paint on iris and pupil, with a faint line in brown over the top of the white. Hair should be in a middle tone of the colour required, with darker and lighter tones added and blended in.

One of the other difficult jobs is shadow. The beginner would do well to keep this to a minimum until he has gained some experience, but basically a figure will cast its own shadows on the folds and creases of its covering and these can be used as guide lines. On a well modelled figure the paint can be brushed until it collects in the hollows and so creates its own highlights and shadows, the white undercoat or light colour of the plastic showing beneath the colour for the highlights. If it is necessary to paint in shadow and highlights always use darker and lighter shades of the basic colour for that area, not black and white. Horses are usually extremely well made, even the veins standing out, and the brushing method is again the best way of forming natural highlights and shadows. An alternative is to paint the horse, then lightly remove some of the paint with a piece of sponge: this will pick out the raised parts for highlights and leave the depressions in a darker tone for shadow.

'Leather' parts can be made to look more lifelike by using a matt paint and when thoroughly dry rubbing carefully with a minute amount of grease, such as vaseline. This is especially effective with black, but I find the grease on your own fingertips is sufficient for brown leather. Dull metallic finishes, such as the Humbrol Gun-metal, also benefit from this treatment. On light-coloured plastic models, or white undercoated metal, 'wooden' parts can be made to look more realistic by wiping some of the paint off while still wet, or by streaking it with a dry brush, thus creating an impression of grain by allowing the material beneath to show through occasionally. This applies mainly to larger areas of wood, such as occur in cannon and other medieval artillery.

One word here about the dreaded 'metal rot' often mentioned in modelling magazines. This is a reaction within the alloy of the figure which can cause the paint finish to be ruined, although the 'disease' is not so common as it would appear from the number of comments on it. Metal rot is aggravated by a cold, damp atmosphere and may therefore be guarded against simply by keeping your models in a warm, dry atmosphere. An undercoat of high polyurethane content varnish will also help.

All the above information applies mainly to 54 mm. scale figures and above but may also be applied to the smaller 30 mm. figures. In the 25 mm., 20 mm. and smaller scales such detail is not really possible or worthwhile, since these scales are normally used by wargamers, where durability is more important than fine detail. Gloss paints, or matt covered by a matt varnish, are really best in these smaller scales, to give the strength needed to withstand constant handling and the stowage conditions between games. Conversion work in these smaller scales is also limited if the pieces are not to fall off during handling, although quite a few changes can be made to plastic figures. There is no adhesive which will securely join the soft plastic used for most of these figures, so pins are the only real answer. (Araldite does join this plastic but often the joint will come apart if the figures are used in wargaming, which I am assuming they will be.) However, heads may be interchanged at will by using pieces of pin, as may the top and lower halves of bodies. It is often best to replace weapons with pin or wire, as they are often much too thick for the scale, or, if thin, so springy that they shed their paint after a few games.

Until recently there was a scarcity of model figures for the medieval period, regardless of scale, but in the last year or so many manufacturers have begun to produce an expanding range of collector's figures for the period. The artillery of the period has received less attention to date. There has also been an increase in the number of metal figures available in wargaming scales, but the plastic range remains limited and many of those produced by Airfix do not readily lend themselves to conversion to different nationalities and eras. The list below gives a rough guide to the range of figures and accessories available at the time of going to press.

150 mm. and above
FOOT. Henry V (Airfix); Joan of Arc (Airfix); Knights (Aurora).
MOUNTED. Knight (Aurora.)

90 mm. by Lippett
FOOT. Knight. (Due out: Crossbowman, Longbowman, Man-at-arms.)
MOUNTED. Knight.

77 mm. by Series 77
FOOT. Landsknechts.
MOUNTED. Knights.

54 mm.
FOOT. Henry V (Stadden); Joan of Arc (Stadden); Richard III (Frontier); Black Prince (Guardhouse, Hinton Hunt); Dauphin (Guardhouse, Hinton Hunt); Knights and men-at-arms (Guardhouse, Hinton Hunt, Jac, Lasset, Rubin, Imrie/Risley); Longbowman (Trophy, Hinton Hunt, Jac, Rose Miniatures); Crossbowman (Guardhouse, Hinton Hunt, Lasset); French Infantry (Guardhouse, Hinton Hunt); English Infantry (Guardhouse); Landsknechts (Trophy, Rose Miniatures); Halberdier (Hinton Hunt, Rose Miniatures); Herald, Billman, Pikeman and Handgunner by Hinton Hunt.
MOUNTED. Knights (Jac, Lasset, Alymer, Trophy Miniatures.)

ARTILLERY. Catapult (Roman) by Old Guard (U.K.) Inc.

25 mm.

FOOT. Men-at-arms (Miniature Figurines, Airfix, Lamming, Garrison); Peasants (Miniature Figurines, Airfix); Crossbowmen (Miniature Figurines, Lamming, Garrison); Armoured Infantry (Miniature Figurines, Airfix); Longbowmen (Miniature Figurines, Airfix, Lamming, Garrison); Halberdier (Miniature Figurines, Warrior Miniatures); Handgunner (Miniature Figurines, Warrior); Pikeman (Miniature Figurines, Warrior, Lamming); Sword-and-buckler man (Warrior); Spearmen, Landsknechts and Standard Bearer by Miniature Figurines.

MOUNTED. Black Prince (Lamming); Knights (Lamming, Garrison, Airfix, Miniature Figurines); Herald, Arquebusier and Hungarian Hussar by Miniature Figurines.

ARTILLERY. Ballista (Lamming, Garrison, Miniature Figurines); Catapult (Lamming, Garrison, Miniature Figurines); Mangonel (Hinchliffe); Bombard and crew (Lamming); Mons Meg, Wallgun, Field gun and Organ gun (ribauldequin) by Miniature Figurines.

1/300 (6 mm.) by Skytrex

FOOT. Knights, Spearmen, Crossbowmen, Longbowmen.
MOUNTED. Knights.
ARTILLERY. Ballista and crew; Ram and crew; Sow; Trebuchet; Fifteenth century siege cannon; Mantlets; Scaling ladder and crew.

1/360 (5 mm.) by Leicester Micro-Models

FOOT. Knights, Spearmen, Crossbowmen, Longbowmen, Peasants.
MOUNTED. Knights; Light Cavalry.
ARTILLERY. Trebuchet; Cat; Siege tower; Mantlets; Fortifications.

APPENDIX TWO

Wargaming in the Medieval Period

THERE is not space in this book to do an 'in depth' study of wargaming itself and I must perforce assume that readers interested in this appendix are familiar with the basics of the hobby. Newcomers to the hobby will find an introduction to the basics of wargaming in such books as *Wargames* by Don Featherstone, published by Stanley Paul; *Discovering Wargames* by John Tunstill, published by Shire Publications; and my own *An Introduction to Battle Gaming*, published by Model and Allied Publications. It should be pointed out that none of these books deals specifically with the medieval period, but to my knowledge nor does any other book on the hobby. Neither are detailed studies of rules specifically for the medieval period as yet very numerous. The best known are *Wars of the Roses* by Ed Smith in the Decalset series of Rules for Wargamers; *1500–1600* by a Birmingham Group of wargamers, published in the same series; and *Rules for Medieval Wargames* by Tony Bath, available from Wargamers' Newsletter, 69 Hill Lane, Southampton, SO1 5AD. Don Featherstone has also given some useful hints in his book *Poitiers 1356* published in the Knight's 'Battles for Wargamers' series by Charles Knight & Co Ltd.

However, before plunging into the rules, the first consideration should be the organisation of the wargames army itself, and here we immediately run into difficulties. The chapter on tactics illustrates how the longbow, pike, wagenburg and correct use of field artillery revolutionized warfare, namely the defeat of heavy cavalry by light or medium infantry. Whilst one would wish to re-enact such victories as Crécy, Mortgarten, Prague and Formigny on the wargames table, obviously it would be unfair and even uninteresting in the long run if one player were always to be the English or the Swiss, and even with the players taking it in turns to have the new weapons, the Swiss would still always win, while the English and Hussite armies would tend to be constantly on the defensive if they were to survive. So one must first make a choice of era within the 1300–1500 period which will equal out the odds somewhat and provide a more interesting game. For example, facing the Swiss pikes with pikes and Spanish sword and buckler men, or English bowmen with efficient field guns and hand guns. The alternatives are to construct a pair of more evenly balanced armies, or to choose to fight only reconstructions of actual battles. Take for instance the proportion of each type of fighting man within an English army of the fourteenth century. Here, on average, there were five archers to every two men-at-arms and every two spearmen or other troops, making at least half the force longbowmen. On the other hand the French usually had about one crossbowman to every three men-at-arms and every four peasants. To field such proportions on a wargames table, even if the English were the attackers, would almost always prove disastrous to the French, who would be swept from the board by massive archery volleys before ever getting to grips. Yet if we were to reduce the number of archers too drastically the small force of English cavalry would be swamped by the French chivalry. Obviously we must choose between reality and enjoyment, or in the terms of the hobby, between serious-minded miniature warfare and just plain wargaming for fun. I make no excuses for belonging to the latter class, but trust that members of the former will still find food for thought in some of my suggestions.

But may we not reach the compromise so important a part of wargaming itself? Let us take a closer look at how these armies were made up. During the Hundred Years War the English armies consisted of men-at-arms, hobilars, spear or bill men, archers, and various smaller bodies of household cavalry, archers of the guard, city militia, Welsh spearmen, engineers, cannoneers, miners etc. The French had men-at-arms, hobilars, mercenary crossbowmen, the peasant levy, and the same assortment of smaller units as the English, with Scottish spearmen instead of Welsh spearmen. These different types of soldiers may be classified as heavy, medium and light cavalry or infantry, plus the peasant levy, as follows: *Peasant Levy:* French peasantry, including bowmen and spearmen (javelins really) as well as other crude weapons; Welsh spearmen, Irish axemen. All were unarmoured. *Light Infantry:* Engineers, miners, cannoneers, English longbowmen. These wore steel caps and some had jacks or brigandines. *Medium Infantry:* English spear or bill men; Scots spearmen fighting for the French; city militias; mercenary crossbowmen; guard archers. Dress similar to the light infantry, but spearmen and militia carried shields, while the crossbowmen and guard archers may have had better armour – this allows a better performance in keeping with their status. *Heavy Infantry:* dismounted men-at-arms of all ranks on both sides. *Light Cavalry:* hobilars on both sides. Mounted archers and crossbowmen could be introduced, but both were only mounted infantry and did not fight on horseback. On the limitations of a wargames table it would not be fair to introduce their mobility as a factor, although they would be important if playing a campaign. *Medium Cavalry:* men-at-arms of the rank of squire and sergeant, their horses unarmoured and the men lightly armoured in comparison with – *Heavy Cavalry:* knights and above – heavily armoured men and horses. In my own army for this period the forces are proportioned as below:

English	Arm	French
10	Heavy Cavalry	20
30	Medium Cavalry	40
10	Light Cavalry	10
60	Heavy Infantry	100
40	Medium Infantry	110
135	Light Infantry	75
———		———
285		355*

(*Peasant levies are added when extra numbers are called for on the French side owing to terrain difficulties during attack etc.)

From these figures you can see that, including ten guard archers in the medium infantry total, the English force still has fifty per cent of its number in archers (Light Infantry), but the difference between the French and English medium and heavy cavalry has been reduced to a 3:2 ratio to give a chance of some cavalry action. To counter their high ratio of archers in the Light Infantry category, the English force is heavily outnumbered in all other categories, as it would have been in real life.

This sort of balance is more difficult to achieve in the various internal wars of the Holy Roman Empire during the same period, where the new tactics of the Swiss and Hussites overwhelmed the feudal cavalry and levy, but some balance can be achieved by superior numbers on the German side or, better still, by 'raising' your army after 1450, when hand-gunners can be employed, and by c. 1475 some Land-sknechts also, to give approximately equal chances of victory on the table. Of course, the rules will need to be 'loaded' so that when feudal cavalry do charge home successfully the effect is devastating, and we will deal with rules now. Please bear in mind that what follows is an out-line only, to give the beginner something from which to build, and the rules and ideas are deliberately sketchy. It is not my intention to put forward a set of rules as *the* rules for the period: these ideas are the bones of my original set, but I know only too well from the internal strife within my own group of wargaming friends, that each player adds the fat and the muscle to the bones according to his own prejudices, however innocent those prejudices might be!

Movement

Light Infantry and Levies 200 mm.

Light Cavalry 300 mm.

Medium Infantry 150 mm.

Medium Cavalry 250 mm.

Heavy Infantry 100 mm.

Heavy Cavalry 200 mm.

Wagons, siege engines and cannon 100 mm.

1) ARTILLERY. Once placed in position siege engines and cannon may not be moved.

2) CHARGE MOVES. Add 100 mm. to light, 75 mm. to medium and 50 mm. to heavy troops for charge moves.

3) ROADS. 50 mm. added to all move distances when in column (three abreast) on roads. It should be borne in mind that roads were few and far between at this date, and did not resemble our notion of roads.

4) FORMATION. Changing formation takes a move. Units may not change formation if within missile or charge range of the enemy.

5) DIRECTION. When changing direction no figure may move more than the maximum distance for the arm concerned. No other restrictions.

6) OPEN ORDER. Peasant levies, light infantry and light cavalry may operate in open order (25 mm. between figures.)

7) OBSTACLES. Deduct a third of a move when climbing hills, or crossing a wall, hedge or fence. Deduct half a move to cross streams and marshes. Only light troops may climb hills where the contours are between 25 and 50 mm. apart; less than 25 mm. means the hills may not be climbed at all.

236

8) WOODS. Only light troops may pass through woods without becoming unformed. They must remain in open order. Other troops may pass through but become unformed and need half a move to rally on leaving the wood. Infantry move at half speed, cavalry at half the appropriate infantry speed, i.e. heavy cavalry at half heavy infantry rate, it being assumed they must dismount to pass through woods.

Firing (Distances in millimetres)

Weapon	*Long Range*	*Effective Range*	*Short Range*
Longbow	300	200	100
Short bow	250	100	50
Crossbow	300	200	75
Arbalest	350	200	75
Sling	275	200	75
Spear	–	100	50
Handgun and Ribauldequin	400	200	100
Culverin	500	250	150 (Canister)
Bombard	350	200	150 (Canister)
Ballista	300	200	Not applicable
Mangonel	400	250	Not applicable
Trebuchet	500	350	Not applicable

1) CANISTER. Use a wire frame, 150 mm. long, starting at the cannon mouth, spreading to 50 mm. wide at 50 mm. from the cannon, then tapering to a point again. Lay this over the figures in the path of the fire and remove fifty per cent of those within the frame. Any doubtful figures and officers may be saved by a throw of 4, 5 or 6 on a dice.

2) ARTILLERY. Siege engines and cannon may only be fired every third move. Ribauldequins may only be fired once in a game.

3) LONG AND SHORT BOWS may fire three times a move, or take 1/3rd move and fire two, or 2/3rds move and fire once. One volley is fired before receiving other fire, the middle volley corresponds with fire from other sources, and the third volley is fired after deducting casualties inflicted by other fire.

4) CROSSBOWS AND ARBALESTS may fire once per move, or may move, but may not move *and* fire. (There should really be some limit on the number of volleys possible for all forms of bow, though this does cause a great deal of 'staff work' if companies fire at different rates and at different times. A table can be used, or counters placed beside each unit. Making allowance for the retrieval of arrows, 20 volleys strikes a reasonable balance.)

5) SPEARS (this meaning the javelins of the peasantry and light infantry, not the spears of the medium infantry) may fire only twice in a game unless confronted by other spearmen, when missiles may be returned until a decision is reached or the action broken off. In the case of the latter, units still operational are considered to have only one spear per man for the next encounter. Spear men may take a full move, or half a move and throw one spear, or throw both spears without moving.

6) HANDGUNS may only fire twice in every three moves and may not move if firing.

7) NUMBER OF RANKS FIRING. English archers may fire four ranks deep if en herse, otherwise all firing is restricted to the front two ranks unless positioned on the forward slope of a hill, when all ranks may fire over the heads of the rank in front.

8) CASUALTIES. Half a dice score for every five men firing at long range; one dice score at effective range; two dice

scores at close range. If firing at light troops in close order take casualties as dice score. At light troops in open order and medium troops the score is halved; at heavy troops only one-third of the score is taken. Fractions over half are rounded up, under half discounted. To decrease the fractions all dice taken for one target have their scores added together before halving etc. Casualties from artillery are taken on the same basis, one dice for each weapon, except that armour provides no extra protection and therefore all troops count as light troops. Handguns at close range and effective range have the same benefit.

9) COVER. Infantry behind hard cover may not be fired on unless they expose themselves to fire back, when all casualty rates are halved.

10) GUARD ARCHERS. Add one to each dice score.

11) COMMANDERS. If firing at an individual figure, such as a lord, a six must be scored to take that figure, otherwise there is no effect from the firing.

Charges and Mêlées

This is a vital sphere of medieval wargaming, for many charges could not be pressed home in the face of intense missile fire or because of spear or pike hedgehogs, while many infantry would not stand up to a cavalry charge once it had penetrated that missile or polearm barrier. A quite intricate system of who will charge whom and who will stand and receive whom is concisely listed in Tony Bath's rules, under 'Hand to Hand Fighting', and I would recommend beginners to follow these rules initially. This system should not be too complex for the beginner, who has to constantly refer to the rules, as the different reactions are neatly set out and can soon be found. The only alternative is a rather clumsy simplification, stating that if more than one degree

of armour separates the units (i.e. heavy cavalry charging
light cavalry, or heavy infantry charging light infantry) the
light troops need to throw a six to stand. If heavy charge
medium then a throw of 4, 5 or 6 is needed. This will
prevent light troops standing alone against the threat of a
heavy charge, as they will almost certainly be massacred if
actually charged, and may encourage players to give decent
support to the light troops or withdraw them to that
support when such a threat is becoming obvious. However,
this does not deal with all the complications, such as light
cavalry charging medium infantry and so on, as do Tony
Bath's rules. On the other hand his rules cannot and do not
cover all eventualities for battles during the years covered
by this book, being primarily designed for simplicity. For
example, they are rather unbalanced for heavy infantry
against heavy cavalry (Rule 18) and do not allow for the
infantry polearms which had such a decisive effect on any
cavalry charge. Medium infantry such as Scottish and
Flemish spearmen, English billmen, Swiss pikemen and the
Landsknechts simply did not break up when charged: as we
have seen they did exactly the opposite, for their own safety.
If they could be broken up by missile fire then they might
be charged and severely cut up, but if they were intact, or
reasonably so, it would be the heavy cavalry which suffered
if it insisted on charging in. This point illustrates how difficult it is to write in general terms on rules, and is not a
criticism of Tony Bath's rules as such, which are thoroughly
recommended as a basis on which to build your own rules.
Obviously the rules for armies employing Swiss pikes or
German arquebuses will need to be vastly different from
those using the early fourteenth century spearmen and
crossbowmen combination, or the English longbow. I can
only suggest that in the field of charges and mêlées you
develop the rules appropriate for your armies from Tony
Bath's basic set, or one of the other sets listed above, and
make use of the tactical and weapon capability details
included in this book.

Additions could be made to the mêlée rules. For example, units caught unformed or those pursued could suffer the penalty of their attackers doubling their dice scores. There should really be a system of rallying moves: light troops mêlée freely, breaking formation, and therefore need a move to rally afterwards: medium and heavy infantry never break ranks and need only half a move to rally: heavy cavalry break ranks to mêlée but need only half a move to rally.

Since much of the fighting in the 1300–1500 period still had an emphasis on ransom as far as the chivalry was concerned, any man-at-arms unit losing a mêlée could surrender ten per cent of its surviving number as prisoners. Any officers could throw a 5 or 6 to see if they were excluded from this number.

Morale

Because the leaders were so important in medieval times we need rather different rules for morale in this period. If the lord in command of a Battle falls or is taken, a dice should be thrown for all the men under his command. 1 = surrender. 2 = run. 3 = refuse to advance. 4 = fighting withdrawal. 5 and 6 = fight on. If the lord of a unit within a Battle falls or is taken his retinue must dice as above. If the commander-in-chief falls or is taken then *each* Battle must dice as above.

Any unit, except those listed below, which is reduced to fifty per cent or less of its original strength must leave the board, unless rallied by a Banneret or above. Throw a 4, 5 or 6 to stay each move, and the Banneret or other officer must remain with the unit. If he leaves, the unit must run. When losing the dice throw to stay, the unit and officer retreat their normal move.

Guard archers, household cavalry and Swiss pikemen fight to the last man. Heavy cavalry and heavy infantry may fall to one-third of their original strength before leaving the field.

Further Suggestions

One addition to the above rules which gives a tang of medieval atmosphere to a game is dicing before setting out your troops to see if they all arrive on the start line. For example, do all the lords and their retinues answer the call to arms in the first place? Do any nobles and their following leave the field because of intrigue or treason? In the fifteenth century only, do any mercenaries leave because they have not been paid, or desert to the enemy for higher pay? These matters can be easily decided by a throw of two dice – say 2 to leave the board, 3 to desert to the enemy. This element of chance can unbalance the best of forces and provides a more interesting game.

Siege operations are really a field in their own right, but basically the rules can be very simple. Stretches of wall, towers and gates are all given numerical values indicating their strength. Each hit with a stone removes a certain number of value points, the scale varying according to the type of weapon, size of stone and range, until zero value is achieved and a breach effected. Mining has to be conducted on paper, at so many inches per move. Counter-mining and listening posts must also be on paper, and an umpire is therefore needed to review every move the plans of both players to see if the listeners or miners can hear any mining work by the enemy. Fire in the form of incendiary arrows is subjected to the usual firing rules, plus a 50-50 chance of catching the target alight and surviving the attempts of the enemy to extinguish it. Fires can only be extinguished, of course, if the men can survive any covering fire.

Further developments, for both siege warfare and open warfare, are apt to be individualistic, and are best arrived at from experience gained during actual games fought in the period which you favour. All I will add therefore is – good luck!

SOURCES

THERE are many books available which deal specifically with such subjects as castles, heraldry, medieval weapons and armour; a lesser number which concentrate on tactics of the era and the feudal system; and a very few which cover the remaining subjects dealt with in this book, namely siege warfare and the raising and organisation of medieval armies. However, it is surprising how few of these books contain any great amount of information on the 1300–1500 period. Because of this, the following bibliography of my main sources for each subject is rather short. Needless to say, a great deal of information was also gathered from other works, most of which do not deal specifically with the 1300–1500 period, or even with medieval armies in particular. These have not been included, since many are now out of print and not readily available for study, but it is hoped that the reader will find sufficient references to these works within my main sources and may take his own investigations from that point.

Of course, using books readily available as a main source means that we are not dealing with the primary sources of information, but fortunately in most European countries there is a wealth of information in other forms which, although ancient, is reliable. I refer to such sources as the numerous surviving castles, town defences and monuments, and the treasure houses of the churches, universities and national museums, wherein may be found examples of weapons and armour of our period, and medieval manuscripts and seals illustrating armorial bearings, armour, weapons, fortifications, siege warfare and tactics. These primary sources are especially valuable in the field of armour, for very little armour has survived for the period before 1450, and most of our information comes from tomb effigies, illuminated manuscripts and seals. These primary sources may be found throughout Europe and most are accessible to all with the curiosity to track them down.

BIBLIOGRAPHY

Chapter 1: The Feudal System and Organisation of Armies
Cutts, Rev. E. L. *Scenes and Characters of the Middle Ages*. Virtue
& Co.
Featherstone, D. *Poitiers, 1356*. Charles Knight & Co., 1972.
Fisher, H. A. L. *A History of Europe*, Vol. 1. Fontana, 1972.
Hibbert, C. *Agincourt*. Batsford 1964, Pan, 1968.
Keen, M. *The Pelican History of Medieval Europe*. Penguin, 1973.
Norman, Vesey. *The Medieval Soldier*. Arthur Barker, 1971.
Norman, Vesey, & Pottinger, D. *Warrior to Soldier*. Weidenfeld
& Nicolson, 1966.

Chapter 2: Armour
Cutts, Rev. E. L. *Scenes and Characters of the Middle Ages*. Virtue &
Co.
Ellacott, S. E. *Armour and Blade*. Abelard-Schuman, 1962.
Mann, Sir J. *Outline of Arms and Armour in England*. H.M.S.O.,
1969.
Norman, Vesey. *Arms and Armour*. Weidenfeld & Nicolson, 1969.
Norman, Vesey, & Pottinger, D. *Warrior to Soldier*. Weidenfeld
& Nicolson, 1966.
Wilkinson, F. *Arms and Armour*. Hamlyn, 1969.

Chapter 3: Weapons
Cutts, Rev. E. L. *Scenes and Characters of the Middle Ages*. Virtue
& Co.
Ellacott, S. E. *Armour and Blade*. Abelard-Schuman, 1962.
Norman, Vesey, & Pottinger, D. *Warrior to Soldier*. Weidenfeld
& Nicolson, 1966.
Rogers, Col. H. C. B. *Artillery through the ages*. Seeley Service,
1971.
Wilkinson, F. *Edged Weapons*. Guiness Signatures, 1970.
Wise, T. *European Edged Weapons*. Almark, 1974.

Chapter 4: Tactics
Cutts, Rev. E. L. *Scenes and Characters of the Middle Ages*. Virtue
& Co.

Fuller, J. F. C. *Decisive Battles of the Western World*, Vol. 1. Eyre & Spottiswoode, 1954.

Oman, C. W. C. *The Art of War in the Middle Ages*, revised J. H. Beeler. Cornell University Press, 1968.

Preston, R. A., Wise, S. F., & Werner, H. O. *Men in Arms*. Thames & Hudson, 1962.

Rogers, Col. H. C. B. *Artillery through the ages*. Seeley Service, 1971.

Sellman, R. R. *Medieval English Warfare*. Methuen Outlines, 1970.

Smail, R. C. *Crusading Warfare*. Cambridge University Press, 1956.

Treece, H. & Oakeshott, E. *Fighting Men*. Brockhampton Press, 1963.

Chapter 5: Castles and other Fortifications

Brown, R. Allen. *English Medieval Castles*. Batsford, 1954.

Hindley, G. *Castles of Europe*. Hamlyn, 1968.

Turner, H. L. *Town Defences in England and Wales*. John Baker, 1971.

Warner, P. *The Medieval Castle*. Arthur Barker, 1971.

Wise, T. *Forts and Castles*. Almark, 1972.

Chapter 6: Siege Warfare

Brown, R. Allen. *English Medieval Castles*. Batsford, 1954.

Cutts, Rev. E. L. *Scenes and Characters of the Middle Ages*. Virtue & Co.

Warner, P. *The Medieval Castle*. Arthur Barker, 1971.

Wise, T. *Forts and Castles*. Almark, 1972.

Chapter 7: Heraldry

Bouton, V. *Armorial de Gelre*, 7 vols. 1881.

Gayre, G. R. *Heraldic Standards*. Oliver & Boyd, 1959.

Hulme, F. E. *Flags of the World*. Warne, 1908.

Pine, L. G. *International Heraldry*. David & Charles, 1970. (Limited application.)

Planché, J. R. *Pursuivant of Arms*. Chatto & Windus, 1851.

Woodward, Rev. J., & Burnett, G. *Treatise on Heraldry, British and Foreign*. 1894; David & Charles, new edition, 1969.

GLOSSARY

Ailette. A rectangular, circular or diamond shaped piece of leather or parchment laced to the shoulder, possibly to deflect a sword-cut to the neck but more likely decorative, bearing the wearer's coat of arms.

Aketon. Shirt-like garment of buckram stuffed with cotton, worn as padding under a hauberk.

Allure. The path along the top of a castle or town wall, providing access to any part of the wall circuit behind the cover of the parapet.

Arbalest. A crossbow with a steel bow stave.

Arçons. The high, enclosing cantle and pommel of a knight's saddle.

Armet. A closed helmet consisting of the rounded cap of the bascinet with two cheek pieces overlapping at the front when closed.

Arquebus. A matchlock firearm originally manufactured in Germany in the mid-fifteenth century. (From hakenbüsche.)

Arrière-ban. The national militia or shire levy of France.

Aventail. A 'curtain' of mail to protect the neck, suspended from the helmet and reaching to the shoulders.

Bailey. A space or courtyard in a castle, enclosed by a wall.

Bandon (pl. banda). A tactical unit of Byzantine cavalry numbering 450 men.

Barbican. A fortification built outside the castle to protect the main gate.

Bascinet. A fourteenth century open-faced helmet of globular or pointed shape, which extended downwards to protect the cheeks and the back of the neck. An aventail was added *c.* 1320 and a pointed visor after 1350.

Battle. A division of troops commanded by a peer or knight banneret.

Besagues. Circular plates laced to the outside of the elbow joint and front of the shoulder to protect the joints in an armour.

Bevor. A high collar of plate covering the lower half of the face.

Bill. A weapon based on agricultural tools and usually having a hooked blade with spikes at top and rear.

Bombard. A large calibre wrought-iron gun or mortar.

Brigandine. A canvas or leather jacket with small plates of metal stitched inside, popular from *c.* 1340.

Buckler. A small round shield carried by infantry to parry blows.

Burgher. A townsman.

Cabacete. A tall narrow helmet, with a turned-down brim which was drawn up to a point at front and rear, worn by Spanish infantry in the late fifteenth century.

Canton. Small division of territory in Switzerland, similar to the English parish.

Cap-à-pied. From head to foot.

Caparison. Fabric or leather horse covering reaching to the fetlocks and usually entirely covering the animal except for openings for eyes and muzzle.

Cat. Stout, rectangular shed with open sides, mounted on wooden wheels, used to provide cover for men using rams, picks and similar weapons against the masonry of a fortification.

Cervelliere. Simple, globular steel cap originally worn under the coif and helm as an additional protection for the head, but evolving into the bascinet at the beginning of the fourteenth century.

Chanfron. Iron plate to protect a horse's face.

Chevaux-de-frise. Plank or beam covered with iron spikes projecting at all angles, originally designed as a defence against cavalry.

Coif. Mail hood covering the head.

Compagnie di ventura. Company of fortune; a band of mercenaries.

Compagnie d'Ordonnance du Roi. Company of 500 mounted men, 15 of which were formed by the king of France in 1445 to provide a standing army.

Comuni. A free city of northern Italy.

Concentric castle. A castle with at least two circuits of walls, one inside the other, the outer wall lower than the inner one so that archers on the latter could fire over the heads of the men on the outer wall.

Condottiero. Captain of a Compagnie di ventura.

Couter. Cup-shaped defence for the elbow.

Crinet. Laminated plate defence for a horse's neck.

Cuir bouilli. Leather hardened in boiling wax.

Cuisses. Quilted, later plate defences for the thighs.

Culverin. Long-barrelled cannon of cast bronze with a small calibre.

Curtain Wall. Stretch of wall in a castle's or town's defences which links the towers.

Drum Tower. A round or half-round flanking tower with very thick walls and plinth.

Echelon. Units of an army regularly stepped back and to one side of the one in front.

Espringale. Medieval term for the Roman ballista, a small engine for throwing spears or stones by means of tension and a large bow stave.

Esquire. See *Squire*.

Estoc. Long, stiff and sharply-pointed sword for thrusting at the joints in plate armour, first introduced in the second half of the fourteenth century.

Falchion. Short, curved, single-edged sword with a broad blade, used for cleaving blows.

Fauld. Skirt of overlapping lames riveted to leather and protecting the wearer below the waist.

Fee. A fee was an estate, sublet to a knight by a baron, bishop or abbot, tenant-in-chief to the king.

Forlorn hope. Assault or storming party with little hope of success, or if successful, little hope of survival.

Free Company. Band of mercenaries formed for the Hundred Years War in France but subsequently fighting in many other parts of Europe.

Fuller. Broad groove running down the centre of each side of some sword blades.

Gambeson. Quilted linen jacket stuffed with flax or rags, worn as a body defence by infantry and over the hauberk by poor knights and sergeants.

Gorget. Plate defence covering the throat, meeting the breastplate at the shoulders and chest.

Greaves. Plate defence for the lower leg.

Halberd. Axe-headed polearm, usually with a rear and top spike.

Hand-and-a-half sword. Large, double-edged sword with a long grip which could be wielded with either one or two hands.

Haubergeon. Shortened version of the hauberk, worn by both infantry and mounted men, those for the former usually having short sleeves.

Hauberk. Mail shirt covering the body as far as the knees, the arms ending in mittens, and with a hood for the head.

Heater shield. Semi-cylindrical shield with a flat top edge. The shield was about 95 cm. long in the first half of the fourteenth century but was shortened later in the century.

Hedgehog. A usually oval formation of several ranks of spearmen presenting a hedge of spear points to any attacker.

Hoardings. Wooden galleries erected on the face of a castle's battlements to enable the defenders to fire on men attacking the base of the wall.

Hobilar. Unarmoured spearmen or archers mounted on a poor breed of horse and used as scouts and despatch riders.

Jack. Canvas or leather jacket reinforced by metal or horn plates stitched between the layers of material.

Jupon. Sleeveless, hip-length garment of leather or padded textile worn over a knight's armour and blazoned with his coat of arms.

Keep. Strong tower within the walls of a castle, used to make a last stand when all other parts of the castle defences had fallen.

Kettle hat. Strong yet light open-faced helmet popular with both knights and infantry throughout the 1300–1500 period, having a conical crown and wide brim.

Knuckle bow. The front half of a sword's crossguard when it turns down towards the pommel to provide a guard for the knuckles.

Laager. Circle of wagons forming a defence for a camp.

Lames. Narrow overlapping plates used to make the flexible parts of an armour.

Landsknechts. German mercenaries organised and equipped in imitation of the Swiss pikemen.

Langets. Narrow iron strips nailed to each side of the top of a staff weapon's haft to prevent the head of the weapon being chopped off.

Liege lord. The principal lord, or tenant-in-chief, to whom knights rendered their service in exchange for land.

Livery. The tunic worn by a servant or follower of a lord, being in the colours of the lord's arms and bearing his badge.

Long sword or sword of war. A hand-and-a-half sword.

Machicolation. Parapet built out on corbels so that missiles could be hurled through the aperture so created to prevent men attacking the base of a wall.

Man-at-arms. Any mounted fighting man who wore armour.

Mangonel. Siege engine operated by the torsion principle and capable of throwing a 300-pound stone up to 400 yards.

Maul. Long handled mallet often carried by English longbowmen and used as both a weapon and a tool.

Money-fief. Military service rendered in exchange for an annual payment from the king.

Morning Star. Five foot long club, its head studded with iron spikes, used by the Swiss during the 1300–1500 period.

Pauldron. Large curved plate worn in pairs to protect the front and rear of the shoulder, replacing the spaudler at the end of the fourteenth century.

Pavise. Large rectangular shield carried by spearmen or shield bearers (pavisers) and used to provide cover for crossbowmen.

Peytral. Breastplate for a horse.

Pike. Long spear with small iron head.

Placate. Narrow plate rising to a point in the middle of the top edge, worn below a shortened breastplate to allow more flexibility.

Poleaxe. Staff weapon with axe-head, balanced by a rear spike or hammer head and with spikes at the top and bottom of the haft. Used by dismounted knights.

Poleyn. Small plate defence covering the knee cap and extending down the shin.

Pommel. Knob at the top of a sword-hilt, counterbalancing the weight of the blade.

Quillons. Iron bar forming the crossguard of a sword or dagger.

Rerebrace. Plate defence for the upper arm.

Retinue. Small troop of fighting men of all types raised on the estate of a knight.

Ribauldequin. Several small calibre cannon clamped on a wheeled platform to form a primitive quick-firing gun.

Ricasso. Blunt part of a sword blade immediately above the cross-guard.

Sabaton. Mail or laminated plate defence for the foot.

Sallet. Helmet with a fixed or pivoted visor and extended 'tail' to protect the neck, worn by both infantry and mounted men in the fifteenth century. It was often worn in conjunction with a bevor.

Scale armour. Small rectangular plates of horn, sometimes metal, attached to a leather or linen coat. Lighter and more flexible than mail.

Schiltron. A usually oval formation of several ranks of spearmen presenting a hedge of spear points to any attacker.

Sergeant. Mounted and armoured soldier below the rank of knight.

Sergeant-at-arms. Member of a royal bodyguard.

Sheaf arrow. Heavy armour piercing arrow used by longbowmen at close range.

Shire levy. All able-bodied men between the ages of 16 and 60, called out in times of national crisis by the king.

Signori. Feudal lords, or local tyrants, in Italy.

Spaudler. Curved plate defence for the shoulder, divided into several lames for greater flexibility.

Squire. Apprentice knight, aged between 13 and 21, classed as a man-at-arms in action.

Surcoat. Long, loose, sleeveless gown worn over a knight's armour.

Tabard. Short, loose garment, open at the sides and having short, wide sleeves, worn from *c.* 1425 by some knights.

Targe. Round or oval shield used by infantry and occasionally by knights.

Tassets. Triangular plates suspended from a shortened fauld after *c.* 1430, protecting the joint with the cuisses yet allowing greater flexibility.

Tenure. In the medieval sense the holding of a piece of land by giving military service to the possessor of the land.

Trapper. Textile or leather covering for a horse, reaching to the fetlocks and usually entirely covering the animal except for openings for eyes and muzzle.

Trebuchet. The largest type of siege engine, hurling boulders by the counter-poise system.

Two-handed sword. Large, double-edged sword with a long hilt to enable it to be swung with two hands. Popular with the Swiss and Landsknechts.

Vambrace. Plate defence for the forearm.

Vasi. The first small, cast brass cannon, *c.* 1325.

Vassal. Feudal tenant who vowed obedience to his lord and in return held land under him.

Wagenburg. Fortified and highly trained version of the ordinary wagon laager, capable of rapid manœuvring and impregnable against cavalry. Developed by the Czechs against the forces of the Holy Roman Empire in the fifteenth century.

INDEX

(Numbers in italic refer to illustrations: the word arms refers to armorial bearings or coats of arms.)

Agincourt, 9, 25, 27–9, 76, 117–19, 214, *118*

ailette, 35

aketon, 37–8

Amieira castle, 154

Angers castle, *143*

Angoulême, Counts of, badge, 217

Anjou, Dukes of, 12; arms, *209*; crest, *209*

Anvin family, arms, 200, *201*

Aragon, King of, arms, *211*; crest, *211*

arbalest, 88–90

Arbedo, battle of, 123–4, 126

archers: equipment of, 40, 58; mounted, 19, 22

Archers of the King's Guard, 24

armet, 55, *56*

armies, 1; Bohemian, 18

    English, 9, 17, 25–6

    French, 15–16, 23, 26

    Hussite, 18, 24–5, 27

    Spanish, 15, 25–6

    Swiss, 17, 24, 26–7

armour: cost, 58; manufacture, 49; manufacturing areas, 49–50; styles, 50, 54, *51*; weight, 48–9

arquebuse, 17, 102–3, 129

arriere-ban, 3, 10

arrows, 91–2

Arundel, Sir John, arms, 200, *199*

augmentation of arms, 207

Austin family, arms, 196, *195*

Austria, King of, arms, *211*; crest, *211*

Auvergne, Counts of, arms, 200, *201*

aventail, 37, 46, 55

Avignon, walls of, 155

Avila, walls of, 154, *156*

axe, 79–81, *78, 79, 83*

backplates, 42, 50, 54, *52*

Baden, banner of, *219*

badges, 212–13, *215, 217*

Balbi-Porto family, arms, 192, *195*

ballista, 164–5

ballock knife, 84, 86

banners, 216–18, *219, 220*

Bannockburn, battle of, 20, 23, 111

barbican, 146, *144*

barbute (helmet), 37, *43*

bardiche, 82

Barre, Count of, arms, 200, *199*

bascinet, 37, 46, 55, *44, 48*

Basset, Lord, arms, 194, *195*

battering ram, 170

Battle (unit), 20, 26

Bavaria, Duke of, arms, *209*; crest, *209*

Beauchamp, Earls of Warwick, arms, 196, *197*

Bedford castle, siege of, 163

belfry, 174–6, *173*

Berg, Barons of, arms, 194, *195*

Bertram family, arms, 196, *197*

besagues, 34

bevor, 36, 46, 55, 57

bills, 81, *83*

blockading a castle, 163, 177–82, *180*

bodyguard, royal, 4, 24

Bohemia, King of, arms, *211*; banner, *219*; crest, *211*

Bohun, Earls of Essex, livery, 214

boiling oil, 177

Bouillon, Dukes of, arms, 192, *193*

Bourbon, House of, badge, 217; livery, 214

bow, long, 90–1, *179*; effectiveness, 41, 91, 120; origin, 110; range, 92

bow, short, 93
Brabant, Dukes of, arms, *211*; crest, *211*
    Geoffroi de, arms, 208, *203*
Brandenburg, Margraves of, arms, *209*; crest, *209*
brattice, 142
breach-piece, 172
breastplate, 38–9, 41–2, 50, 54, *53*
Briesen family, arms, 191, *193*
brigandine, 40
Brittany, Dukes of, badge, *217.*
Burgundy, Dukes of, arms, *209*; crest, *209*
Bussnang, Barons of, arms, 194, *195*
Byzantine tactics, 108–9, *108*

cabacete, 57
cadency, 204–6
Caerphilly castle, 146, *147*
Calabria, Dukes of, arms, 196, *197*
Cammer family, arms, 204
Cammerberg family, arms, 204
canister, 98
cannon, *95*, *99*, *100*, *175*, *176*; brass, 94–5; bronze, 98; case shot, 98–9; carriages, 97–8, 101; powder, 97; projectiles, 96, 98–9; ranges, 99; in sieges, 160, 167–8; wrought-iron, 95–6
Canterbury, Westgate, *159*
Carcassonne, walls of, 155, *156*
Carew, Nicholas, arms, 198, *199*
case shot, 98
Castile and Leon, King of, arms, *211*; crest, *211*; standard, *219*
castles, *137*, *140*, *141*, *142*, *143*, *144*, *147*, 149, *152–3*, *155*; concentric, 146; decline of, 149–50; European, 151–4; 14th century, 148–50; role of, 134–5
cat (siege weapon), 169–70, *171*
catapult, 165
cavalry: constabulary, 20; lance (unit), 19; light cavalry, 22; organisation, 19–22; tactics, 107–9
cervelliere (helmet), 37
Chandos, Sir John, 20; arms, 192, *195*

chanfron, 64, *60*
Château Gaillard, 139, *141*
Châteaubriand family, arms, 207
Chepstow castle, 148
Chester, Earls of, arms, 200, *201*
Chidiok, Sir John, arms, 196, *197*
cinquedea dagger, 87, *86*
Clarence, Duke of, badge, *215*
Cleeves, Counts of, arms, 202, *201*
Clermont, Marshal of, arms, *209*; crest, *209*
commanders, 8, 9, 11, 15, 19–21, 23–4, 27, 106
Compagnies d'Ordonnance du Roi, 15, 23
Companies of Fortune, 11
Comunidades, 14
condottieri, 11, 128–9
constable, 20, 23, 27
constabulary, 20, 24
contract system, 8–9
Cornwall, Earl of, arms, 207
Corti family, arms, 200, *199*
couter, 33, 45
Crécy, battle of, 25, 112–16, *113*
crest (helmet), 208, 210, *209*, *211*
Crevecoeur family, arms, 196, *197*
crinet, 64, *61*
crossbow, 87–90; bolts and quiver, *89*
crossbowmen, 8, *179*; equipment of, 40, 59; Genoese, 11, 23, 114; proportion in English army, 110
crupper, 64
cuisses, 33
curtain wall defences, 139–42
cyclas coat, 39, 41

Dauphin of France, arms, 200, *199*
Deichsler family, arms, 196, *197*
Della Scala family, 10; Mastino II's arms, *209*; crest, *209*
Derby, Earls of, arms, 188
differencing, 202–3
discipline, 105–6
Douglas, Earls of: livery, 214; standard, *220*
Dunbar, Patrick, arms, 205, *203*
Dupplin, battle of, 112

ear dagger, 84, 87
Ecclesall family, arms, 202
Edward I, King of England, 7, 8; badge, *215*; banner, *220*; livery, 214
Edward III, King of England, 7, 8, 12, 20, 22; arms, *211*; badge, *215*; crest, *211*; livery, 214
Egger, Counts of, arms, 196, *197*
Eltham, John, Earl of Cornwall, arms, 207, *203*
England, arms, 198, *199*; flags, 220; livery, 214
escalade, 174, *181*
espringale, 164–5
esquire, 2, 21–2
Essenau, Soumeret d', arms, 196, *197*
estoc, 70–1, *66*
Exeter, Dukes of, badge, *217*
Eyck family, arms, 192, *193*

falchion, 67, 69–70, *69*, *70*
Falkirk, battle of, 25, 111
fauld, 42, 50–2, *54*
fee, knight's, 2
feudal tenure, 1–2; faults of, 7; in Spain, 14
fief, 2; division of, 6; money fief, 6, 9
Fieschi family, arms, 194, *195*
Fitzwilliam, Ralph, arms, 200, *201*
flanchards, 64
Flanders, Counts of, arms, 198, *199*
Flodden Field, battle of, 20, 98
Florence, arms, 200, *201*
Formigny, battle of, 119–20
fortified manor houses, 150
Franc-archiers, 15
France: arms, *209*; crest, *209*; flags, 220–1; livery, 214; standard, *220*
Free Companies, 12–13
Frigebur, 3
Furnival family, arms, 202

gadlings, 34
Gaillard castle, 139, *141*
gambeson, 22, 38
gate, city, 159–60; Canterbury's, *159*

gatehouse, castle, 145–6
gauntlets, 34, 45, 55, *54*
Geneville family, arms, 200, *201*
Genoa, arms, 192, *193*
Geoffroi de Brabant, arms, 208, *203*
Ghisi family, arms, 191, *193*
Giron family, arms, 196, *197*
gisarme, 82
glaive, 81
gonfannon, 219
Gonzagas, Dukes of Mantua, 10; arms, 192, *195*
gorget, 36, 46
Grandson, battle of, 127, *127*
Granullas family, arms, 200, *199*
grapeshot, 99
greaves, 33
Greek fire, 166–7, 176–7
Grey, John de, arms, 205, *203*
Griffa family, arms, 200, *199*
Guesclin, Bertrand du, 13, 20; arms and crest, *209*
guidon, 218–9
gunpowder, 97

Hainault, Counts of, badge, *217*
Hainault, Duke of, arms and crest, *211*
halberd, 82, 124, *83*
hand-and-a-half sword, 68–9, *69*
handgunners, 132–3, *162*
handguns, 101–3, 130, 132–3, *162*
Hastings, Earls of Huntingdon, arms, 202, *203*
haubergeon, 38
hauberk, 32, 34, 38, *31*
Hauten family, arms, 191, *193*
haute-pieces, 54
Hawkwood, Sir John, 13, 20
Heerban, 3
Henry IV, King of England, standard, *219*
Henry V, King of England, arms, *211*; badges, *215*; crest, *211*; livery, 214
Henry VII, King of England, banners, *220*
heraldry, reasons for, 184–5
heralds, 185

Hermandades, 14
Hilgertshauser family, arms, 204
hoardings, 142, 157, *171*, *180*
hobilar, 19, 22
Hohenstein, Count of, arms, 192, *193*
Holland, Duke of, arms and crest,
  211
Holy Roman Empire: arms, 200,
  209; crest, *209*; flag, 221
horse: numbers involved, 28;
  trappers, 62–5, 214, *61*, *62*, *63*;
  types of, 22–3
household knights, 2, 9, 21
Hoven family, arms, 202, *201*
Hrzistic, Barons of, arms, 192, *193*
Hundred Years War, 12, 13, 16, 22,
  148
Huntingdon, Earls of, arms, 202, *203*
Hussite Wars, 17–18, 130–2

illegitimacy, in heraldry, 206–7
infantry: organisation, 23–6; tactics,
  107–9

jack, 38, 58
Jaffa, battle of, 107–8
jupon, 41, 210, 212

Kalmar castle, 154, *155*
keep: cylindrical, 138; European,
  151–4; of Gaillard castle, *140*; of
  Loches castle, *137*; shell, 136;
  tower, 136–8, *137*; wooden, 135
keep-gatehouse, 145–6
kettle hat, 36, 37, 46, 55
knight bachelor, 20, 216
knight banneret, 20, 216, 218
knight's military service, 4–5, 7, 8
Kossovo, battle of, 132–3
Kulenthal family, arms, 196, *197*

Lancaster, Duke of, 12
lance: *garnis*, 19; rest, 42, 74; type of
  unit, 19; weapon, 74, 76
Landsknechts, 12, 18, 25, 128;
  equipment of, 59, 72
Latimer family, arms, 196, *195*
Laupen, battle of, 122–3

Leicester, Earl of, arms, 200, *201*
Leliwa family, arms, 202, *203*
lettre de retinue, 10
Lewes castle, *144*
Lipan, battle of, 131
livery, 213–14
livery and maintenance, 16
Loches castle, *137*
logistics, 27–8
longbow, 90–1, *179*; effectiveness,
  41, 91, 120; origin, 110; range, 92
longbowmen: equipment of, 40, 58;
  organisation, 24; proportion of,
  110–11; training, 111–12, 117;
  versus longbowmen, 120
Lorraine, Dukes of, arms, 200, *199*
Lowther family, arms, 200, *201*
Lutterell family, arms, 202, *203*

mace, 76–8, *77*, *78*
machicolation, 142, *144*
Magalotti family, arms, 202, *201*
mail: body armour, 30–2, 41, *31*;
  coif, 32, 36; hose, 32, 41; mittens,
  32, 34
Maltravers family, arms, 196, *197*
mangonel, 165
mantlet, 172, *180*
Mantua, Dukes of, arms, 192, *195*
marshal, 27
marshalling, 207–8
Martinet family, arms, 204
matchlock, 102–3
maul, 77
Megenzer family, arms, 191, *193*
men-at-arms, 21
mercenaries: 8–10, 14, 16, 25,
  145; Brabançon, 8, 23, 121;
  Flemish, 103, 127; Gascon, 8, 16,
  128; German, 16, 102, 127, 132;
  Italian, 11, 127; Spanish, 128;
  Swiss, 12, 14, 16, 17, 127
Merseman family, arms, 196, *197*
Milan, Dukes of, 10, 13; badge, *217*
militia: of Florence, 108; in France,
  3, 4, 15; in Germany, 3; in Italy,
  10; national, 3, 4, 7; in Spain, 14
mining, 168–9, 181

moated homesteads, 150
Montferrato, Marquis of, 13; Duke of, arms, 192, *193*
Monti family, arms, 188, *193*
Morat, battle of, *126*
Mortemar, Dukes of, arms, 194, *195*
Mortgarten, battle of, 121–2
motte and bailey castle, 135–6
Motton, Sir William, arms, 200, *201*
mounted archers, 19, 22

Namur, Count of, arms and crest, *209*
Nompar family, arms, 191, *193*
Norfolk, Earl of, Marshal of England; arms and crest, *211*

Orewin Bridge, battle of, 110–11
Orford castle, 138
Orleans, Duke of, 12; badge, *217*
Oxford, Earl of, arms, 204; livery, 214

Parr, Sir John, arms, 206, *203*
Parteneck family, arms, 204, *203*
partition lines, 191–2
partizan, 82
pauldron, 42, 45, 54
Pembroke castle, *142*
pennon, 216
pennoncelle, 216
Percy, Earls of Northumberland: arms, 213; livery, 213; at Shrewsbury, 120; standard, *220*
petard, 177
peytral, 64, *61*
Pierrefeu family, arms, 196, *195*
pike, 84, 122
pixaine, 38
placate, 50, 54
Poitiers, battle of, 12, 25, 71, 116, 185
Poland, kings of, arms, 200, *199*
poleaxe, 76, *75*
poleyn, 32–3
pommel, 68–9, 72
Portugal, King of: arms and crest, *211*; standard, *219*
pourpoint, 38

Queenborough castle, 148–9, *149*
quicklime, as a weapon, 177
quillon dagger, 84, *85*

Rada family, arms, 196, *195*
Raineval, Waleran de, arms, 200, *199*
ram, 170
ranseur, 84
Raventhorpe family, arms, 200, *199*
Reconquista, 14
rerebrace, 33, 45
retinue, 2
ribauldequin, 100–1
ricasso, 71
Richard II, King of England, standard, *220*
Romans, King of the, arms, 200
rondel dagger, 84, 87, *85*
runic shield charges, 202

sabatons, 33, 52, 54
saddlery, 65
Saint Jacob-en-Birs, battle of, 124
sallet, 56–8, *58*, *59*
Santa Hermandad, 14
Sapieha family, arms, 202, *203*
Sart, Counts of, arms, 192, *193*
Sas family, arms, 202, *203*
Savoy, Duke of: arms, *209*; badge, *217*; crest, *209*
Saxony, Duke of: arms and crest, *209*
scabbard, 73–4
scale armour, 32, *61*
scarf (for helmet), 210
Schleich family, arms, 191, *193*
Schwerin family, arms, 196, *197*
Scotland, King of: arms, 196, *199*, *211*; crest, *211*
Scottish Archers of the Guard, 24
scutage, 6
Sempach, battle of, 123
sergeant, 3–4, 21
sergeant-at-arms, 4, 9
sergeanty, 3
shield charges, 192–202
shield money, 6
shields, types: bouché, 45; buckler, 35, 45; heater, 35, 45; kite, 35;

pavise, 36, 45, 47, 172; targe, 36, 45
shire levy, 3–4, 7
Shrewsbury: battle of, 120; Earls of,
   badge, 215; livery, 214
siege tower, 174–6, 173, 178
Silesia, banner, 219
sling, 93–4
slingers, 172
slow match, 100
Somerset, Charles, Earl of Worcester,
   arms, 206, 203
sow (in sieges), 169–70, 171
Spanish infantry: equipment of, 59,
   72; organisation, 25; tactics, 128;
   versus pike, 128
spaudler, 33, 42
spear, 81, 80
spearmen, 8, 9, 40, 71, 81, 87
spur, 33
squire, 2, 21–2
Stafford, Sir Henry: badge, 215;
   standard, 219
Stahleck castle, 152–3
standards, 218, 219, 220
Steps family, arms, 200, 201
stink pots, 177
stirrups, 65
streamer, 219
Stübner family, arms, 194, 195
Suffolk, Dukes of: badge, 217;
   livery, 214
summoning a castle, 161
surcoat, 37, 39, 41, 210
Surrey, Earls of, arms, 196, 197
Swabia, banner, 219
Swiss pikemen: 12, 14, 17, 127;
   equipment of, 59, 72–3; organisation, 124–5; tactics, 122; superiority
   of, 124, 127
Switzerland, flags of cantons, 221

tabard, 212
tassets, 50–2
Tenby, town walls, 158
Tenremonde family, arms, 188, 193
timber forts, 163, 162
tinctures in heraldry, 188, 189; rule
   of, 190–1

Togores family, arms, 200, 201
Toulouse, Counts of, arms, 196, 195
tower, castle, flanking, 142–3, 143;
   city, 157–8, 160
Tower of London, 148
Trappe family, arms, 200, 201
trebuchet, 165–6, 166, 178, 179
Trusbutts family, Barons of Wartre,
   arms, 202, 203
Tuscany, Dukes of, arms, 196, 199
two-handed sword, 72–3

vambrace, 33, 45
Vaux, Sir William, arms, 200, 201
Vere family, Earls of Oxford, arms,
   204, 203
Villehardouin family, arms, 196, 197
Visconti family, Dukes of Milan, 10,
   13; badge, 217
visor, 46, 48
Volz family, arms, 196, 195

wagenburg, 18, 129–31
wages, 9, 28–9
Waldersee, Count of, arms, 192, 195
walled towns and cities, 154–7, 160;
   gates, 159–60; towers, 157–9, 160
Warenne family, Earls of Surrey,
   arms, 196, 197
war-hammers, 78–9, 77
war scythe, 82
Wars of the Roses, 16–17
Wartre, Barons of, arms, 202, 203
Warwick, Earls of: arms, 196, 197;
   badge (on chanfron), 60; livery,
   214
Wells family, arms, 198, 199
Wigtown, Lord of, arms, 202, 203
William of Melun, arms, 208, 203
Worcester, Earl of, arms, 206
wreath (on helmet), 210

Yeomen of the Guard, 24
York, Edward, Duke of, badge, 215;
   Richard, Duke of, badge, 215

Zedwitz, Counts of, arms, 191, 193
Ziska, Jan, 18, 130